DATE DUE

5-31-05			

Demco No. 62-0549

Forever Your Sister

Reflections on Leaving Convent Life

Forever Your Sister

℘ ℭ

Reflections on Leaving Convent Life

Editors

Janice Wedl, O.S.B. and Eileen Maas Nalevanko

NORTH STAR PRESS OF ST. CLOUD, INC.

Library of Congress Cataloging-in-Publication Data

Forever your sister : reflections on leaving convent life / editors,
    Janice Wedl and Eileen Maas Nalevanko.
    160 p. 23 cm.
       ISBN 0-87839-128-2 (pbk. : alk. paper)
       1. Ex-nuns—United States—Biography. 2. Sisters of the Order of
    Saint Benedict (Saint Joseph, Minn.)—Biography. I. Wedl, Janice,
    1929- . II. Nalevanko, Eileen Maas, 1929- .
    BX4668.3.S57F67 1998
    271'.97--dc21
    [B]   98-25707
                                                                      CIP

Cover design: Thomasette Scheeler, O.S.B., and Gail Schlicht.

Cover photography: Thomasette Scheeler, O.S.B.

About the cover: The dome, located over the chapel, is a symbol to all
who pass of the presence, prayer, and profession of the women who have
lived monastic life in the St. Benedict's community for over 140 years.
The leaves, continually changing in size, color, and texture, symbolize
the lives of the women who have come to St. Benedict's Monastery—
those who stayed and those who left—who truly are forever sisters.

All pictures are courtesy the contributors except where otherwise noted.

ISBN: 0-87839-128-2

Printed in the United States of America by Versa Press, Inc., East Peoria,
Illinois.

Published by: North Star Press of St. Cloud, Inc.
                    P.O. Box 451
                    St. Cloud, Minnesota 56302

We dedicate this book

to all former members of
St. Benedict's Monastery, St. Joseph, Minnesota.

May they continue to listen to God
with the ear of their heart
as they proceed on their life's journey.

Table of Contents

*The dates indicate the years the writer spent in the religious community.
Her religious name is also given.*

Foreword

In a letter to us dated February 8, 1997, Pat Pickett, the author of one of the chapters in this book, wrote, "I appreciate all you have done to make this a reality. You should be very proud of the gift you have created which *names* our continued connection. We are different . . . all of us who spent time in community. I have experienced over and over being able to pick out persons who have lived in one community or another. Something does happen. Something did happen which changed all of us forever."

In this book, *Forever Your Sister,* twenty-two women have written of their journeys as they entered and later left St. Benedict's Monastery in St. Joseph, Minnesota. All agree with Pat Pickett that "something did happen which changed all of us forever." The title of the book is taken from the closing sentence Eileen Maas Nalevanko wrote to Sister Linda Kulzer after a reunion weekend for former sisters in 1993. Eileen ended her letter with the words, "Lovingly, and forever your sister."

The women who have written these chapters came to the community for a variety of reasons. One came to please her father who had a drinking problem. He expressed the desire that one of his daughters become a sister and she, at age thirteen, wanting to please him, decided she was the one. Although life in the monastery gave her many opportunities and a level of security, it didn't fit. At the age of forty she realized she had spent too much of her life being a people pleaser. "I was beginning to realize that being a people pleaser while living closely with so many people was destroying me." Another came to fulfill her mother's own thwarted dream of being a sister. After years of knowing religious life was not for her and understanding that her mother's life would not end if she left, she did just that. A Bahamian woman came because she was drawn to what she thought monastic life promised. She found much that was good, but institutional living brought about a feeling of claustrophobia that was not healthy for her. Another found in the Benedictine community a home she had lost after both of her parents had died. Twenty-six years later she left to begin a home of her own with a man she loved. Many young women, particularly if they had attended a Catholic grade or high school, were easily influenced by the suggestion of a priest or sister that they enter religious life but later realized it was not for them. Another, who had attended high school at St. Benedict's, felt that joining the order was certainly the right and best thing a young girl could do to show her love of God. She lived in the community for twenty-five years trying to come to grips with her lack of a religious vocation. Another, who discovered her lesbianism as she became older, realized that she must leave or her spirit would die.

The years spent in the monastery were years of growth for these women. They learned the value and joy of living in community; they received excellent educations; they developed a keen sense of social justice and a love of the liturgy. They followed Benedict's admonishment to "treat all things as the sacred vessels of the altar." They learned skills and wisdom that would continue to serve them well.

Just as they came to the community for a variety of reasons, so they left for a variety of reasons. Several left because they wanted to marry and raise a family. Others left because the religious vocation just "didn't fit." Some left because they were disillusioned with the community or felt their talents and insights were not recognized or appreciated. They left and carried with them the values and the skills and the wisdom they learned while in the community. Above all, they carried with them the love, the loyalty, and the appreciation of those who remained and want to continue to be connected with them.

We are grateful to the women who were willing to share their life stories in these chapters. Others were invited to write but declined. Some of them found that the process of putting their memories into written words was too painful. On the other hand, many who did write were grateful for the task, finding a psychological release in the experience.

While some of the contributors are professional writers, the focus of the chapters is not on scholarship but on communicating one's experiences of living Benedictine values wherever life leads. The chapters are arranged according to the year the authors joined the community.

We ask our readers to peruse this book with reverence. It contains stories of holy women who have listened with the ear of their hearts to the voice of God calling them and have followed this voice on a most mysterious journey.

Janice Wedl, OSB
Eileen Maas Nalevanko
Co-editors
March 21, 1998 Feast of St. Benedict

Acknowledgements

Many people were involved with the publishing of this book. Our initial brain-storming committee of JoAnn Bauer, Beverly Kessler, Doris Nathe Juntilla, Jeannine Schumacher, Eileen Maas Nalevanko, and Janice Wedl, OSB, helped set the stage. Susan Harrison, Sheila Rausch, OSB, Hilda Keller, OSB, Merle Nolde, OSB, Linda Kulzer, OSB, and Norita Lanners, OSB, gave advice on editing and proofing the chapters. Thomasette Scheeler, OSB, assisted with photographs and layout. Thomasette Scheeler, OSB, and Gail Schlicht designed the cover. From the very beginning, members of the monastery's *Studium* supported us by their interest.

The expertise of Kathleen Kalinowski, OSB, was invaluable as she worked out contracts and gave legal and financial advice. It was her suggestion that Sister Ephrem Hollermann, current prioress, be invited to write the introduction. We are grateful to Sister Ephrem for writing such a stellar beginning for our book.

Merle Nolde, OSB, Janice's housemate; John Nalevanko, Eileen's husband; and Linda Kulzer, OSB, friend to both Janice and Eileen, are to be thanked over and over again for their loving support and encouragement throughout the process of bringing this book to fruition.

Rita and Corinne Dwyer, our publishers from North Star Press, supported us all along the way, never letting us lose sight of our purpose. They continually assured us that this book contains a story that needs to be told.

Above all, we thank the twenty-two women who were willing to reflect on their years in our Benedictine community and share in written word how those years have impacted their lives today.

Sister Henrita Osendorf, O.S.B., was an influential person in the lives of almost all of the women who have written chapters for this book. She was novice director from 1943 to 1960, sub-prioress from 1960 to 1961, and prioress from 1961 to 1973. She tried to impress upon the entire community the depth of God's love for each one and she, herself, personified that love. Toward the end of her life, when she realized her memory was failing, her greatest fear was that she might forget how much God loved her. Sister Henrita died on February 12, 1992, at the age of eighty-six. (Courtesy of St. Benedict's Monastery archives)

Introduction

THE TREND WAS SO UNEXPECTED AND DRAMATIC. Between 1963 and 1988 two hundred sixteen women terminated their vowed membership in our community. For some people, a span of twenty-five years may seem like a very long time. But for the sisters of St. Benedict's Monastery in St. Joseph, Minnesota, twenty-five years represents a little less than one-sixth of their 140 year history in central Minnesota—too short a time to be finished with grieving and with attempting to understand the impact of such a "sudden" loss of so many members. Consequently, this is an important book for us.

The women who left our community during those turbulent post-Vatican II decades have themselves journeyed through sagas of confusion and transition and healing to new life. Their journeys, it would seem, were fraught with deeper loneliness than for those of us who remained to ride the winds of change together. A code of silence often surrounded the departures of these women from our midst. It was not the "tenor of the times" to share one's story or to explain one's reason for leaving, much beyond the superior's office. Many of these women left our community without the opportunity to say good-bye to friends and mentors or to experience the healing that closure can bring. This book is for them. In a profound sense it is a voice for the women, "forever our sisters," who have long waited to tell us their stories, to tell us about what was, what has been, and what is, in their lives today.

The stories revealed in these pages represent only a microcosm of what was happening among American Catholic sisters, most dramatically during the 1960s and 1970s. In 1966, membership in religious communities of women in the United States had reached its highest point, peaking at approximately 181,000. Thirty years hence, there has been more than a forty percent decline. There are slightly over 90,000 women religious in the American Catholic Church today. The statistics, however, tell us only a small part of the story.

The 1960s were characterized by enormous change within both Church and society, and few would argue that American Catholic sisters were at the epicenter of change in the church. Those women who had entered religious life prior to 1960 may have thought they were entering into an immutable way of life. Small wonder that a little book could have caught them off guard. In 1962, *The Nun in the Modern World*, by Leon Joseph Cardinal Suenens exploded into their lives. "It has been said of certain congregations of nuns," he said, "that they are the last stronghold of the very studied manners of the middle-class women of the nineteenth century. People would like to see more spontaneity, less inhibition, more natural and straight forward drawing nourishment direct from the earth." As shocking and discounting as these words may seem to us today, they were, along with the mandate of Vatican Council II for the reform and renewal of religious life, taken seriously by American Catholic sisters and heeded conscientiously. For women religious nationwide, the 1960s and 1970s came to be characterized by agonizing self-assessments and re-evaluations in everyday conversation, community meetings, workshops, retreats, and reading lists. At the same time, they were being impacted externally by a cultural upheaval calling for systemic change, heightened social consciousness, political activism, and a new feminism.

I have come to believe in the words of Sherna Gluck in her curiously titled book, that "it is only when individual women talk about their lives that we are able to put the whole story together: the public and the private; the dramatic and the subtle; the gains and the losses" (quoted from "Rosie the Riveter Revisited: Women, War and Social Change" in *Poverty, Chastity and Change* by Carole Garibaldi Rogers). For many years, we who remained in the community at St. Benedict's could only make assumptions about why certain of our members really left during those chaotic years. More recently we came to experience a growing sense of the need to be in contact with these women who had never really left our memories and our hearts. And so we invited our former members to a reunion in the summer of 1993. During those very sacred days, they and we talked about our lives in an effort "to put the whole story together"—the public, the private, the dramatic, the subtle, the gains, and the losses.

Personally, I had never dared to dream of what happened late one night during that reunion weekend, when eight of us who had entered the postulancy together in 1961 were reunited. Assembled in a circle, each of us took a turn to talk about what had transpired in our lives over the previous twenty or so years. I was the only one in the group who had remained in religious life, so the experience was particularly poignant for me. As Polly, Millie, Bernadette, Diane, Judy, Penny, and Ruth told their stories—about marriages, children, careers, widowhood, cancer, joys, sorrows, faith, near loss of faith, love, hope, dreams, and reasons for leaving our community—I was overcome with bittersweet emotions. On the one hand, I remembered my own feelings of abandonment, as one by one twenty-three of the twenty-six women who entered the postulancy with me left between the years 1961 and 1974. I realized how much I still missed them and needed them. On the other hand, I was intensely inspired by their lives and the diverse ways in which each one's search for God was bearing fruit in prayer, work, and service to the people of God all over the country. As I made my way back to my room long after midnight, I knew with certainty that for those who have lived together in the heart of Christ and continue to cling to the desire to seek God, there is no separation, no permanent leave-taking.

Many of us cherish memories of that gathering in August of 1993, but perhaps none so steadfastly as Eileen Maas Nalevanko and Sister Janice Wedl who birthed the idea for this book. Eileen, whose story appears in these pages, recalled that, "The weekend was for all of us a defining moment in our lives. The joyful welcome and embrace of all we had loved became the healing balm for our souls. By the end of that weekend I had shed copious tears, tears of sadness for what I had lost and tears of joy for what I had regained. There was no doubt in my mind. I was forever their sister." Of such sentiments titles of books are born!

Eileen and Janice have collected here stories of some of the women who were once members of St. Benedict's Monastery in St. Joseph, Minnesota, compelled by the conviction that this collective story needs to be told. In these pages you will read about women from Ukiah,

California, to Avon, Minnesota, who left religious life because "this was not God's plan for me" or "my development as a person was at stake" or "I couldn't find my rightful place in the community." You will also learn how their years spent in our Benedictine community became the foundation for maturing in the faith and living a value-centered life. In the following pages you, the reader, will be graced with the wisdom of women like Judith Popp-Anderson, who testifies that the Benedictine "practice of living in the presence of God and receiving others as Christ is a peaceful and positive way to live amid the challenges and struggles of our present culture."

It has been my privilege as current prioress of St. Benedict's Monastery to write this introduction to the stories herein. It is my fervent hope that this book will be received as both a gesture of reconciliation and of celebration—that is, an opportunity for our community to say to all of our former members that "yes" you will be "forever our sisters." May it also be a fitting celebration of women who have had the courage and the strength to follow God's direction in their lives in sometimes unexpected and surprising ways.

Ephrem (Rita) Hollermann, OSB
Prioress
St. Benedict's Monastery
March 1, 1998

Chapter One

Heart Filled with Gratitude

FRANCES HUNKLER ROEHRICH

EVERY WOMAN, REGARDLESS OF THE VOCATION she chooses, would benefit tremendously by having had some experience in monastic life. Saint Benedict describes this life as a "school for the Lord's service," following the Gospel as guide. It is a way of love and a call to holiness of life.

Benedictine community living, with the give and take it demands, offers each member a blessed opportunity for a full and happy life. Monastics live under a rule with an abbot or prioress to lead them. The abbot or prioress is believed to hold the place of Christ in the monastery.

Community members must also have guidelines. Chapter 72 of Benedict's *Rule* states:

School photo of Sister Rhodene Hunkler, 1961.

> *This, then, is the good zeal which members must foster with fervent love. "They should try to be the first to show respect to the other (Romans 12:10)," supporting with the greatest patience one another's weaknesses of body or behavior, and earnestly competing in obedience to one another. No monastics are to pursue what they judge better for themselves, but, instead, what they judge better for someone else. Among themselves they show the pure love of brothers and sisters; to God, reverent love; to their prioress or abbot, unfeigned and humble love.*

1

How did the spirit of Saint Benedict enter into my childhood formation? My childhood days were spent with my twin sister, Mary Jane, near Napoleon, North Dakota, a rural area southeast of Bismarck. We were the youngest of nine children in the Hunkler family.

The oldest in the family, Roy, was instrumental in converting the entire family from the Evangelical Church to Catholicism. At age four, Mary Jane and I met Roy for the first time. Having completed four years as a cleric at Saint John's Abbey, Collegeville, Minnesota, he was then permitted a home visit before continuing his priesthood studies at Assumption Abbey, Richardton, North Dakota.

At this early age Mary Jane and I became deeply influenced by Roy (Father Adam), whom we did not understand to be our brother. Unknowingly, he began to shape the family in a Benedictine way, which remained a motivating factor in our spiritual values. He did this by the joy and enthusiasm he showed in performing his hours of prayer when at home, and his eagerness to return to the abbey. Father Adam had a superior kind of love for each one of us, the kind that attracts others to someone beyond himself. He became my ideal, someone I wanted to emulate in prayer and virtue. A second brother, Father Ignatius, added additional motivation as he, too, entered the Benedictine priesthood.

In our school days, my twin sister and I helped with routine farm chores—milking cows, feeding calves, chickens, and turkeys. Of course, with two minds we thought up a few more pranks than we should have, for example, making mud pies with eggs, mud, and water, until we were questioned about what was happening to all the eggs. Punishment was always lighter because it could be shared. In good deeds and bad, we were always together.

After graduating from Saint Mary's High School, staffed by Benedictine Sisters at Richardton, North Dakota, Mary Jane and I registered for the fall entry at the College of Saint Benedict, St. Joseph, Minnesota. With fearful anticipation we arrived by Greyhound bus at this awesome place, one that we would call our home. This was scary enough; however, motivated by family influence, we also came with the determination that some day we would both join the Benedictine sisters. To our surprise we learned that we could attend college and begin our formation into the sisterhood at the same time. With very little persuasion we were fitted with the black uniform that marked us distinctly as future nuns, while attending college classes. Because we already had music training, we were accepted into the music department, one of the strongest majors of the college.

My twenty-two years in monastic life at Saint Benedict's began at this point, in September 1942. In the spring of 1944, both of us entered the novitiate, a formative year of intense study, prayer, silence, daily Eucharist, community praise, meditation, almost no communication with the rest of the community and none with the outside world. At this time, each novice chose a name to designate her religious identity. Naturally, as twins would do, we chose "twinnish" names, Rhoda and Rhodene.

During our novitiate, we were confronted with a unique experience. An independent priory would be founded in Bismarck, North Dakota. Each sister was to choose either to remain at Saint Benedict's or to be part of the new priory in North Dakota. Novices were directed to pray and make the decision secretly. This was a stressful moment for my sister and me. What if one went and the other stayed? How did this all turn out? There were eight novices from North Dakota, and all eight of us chose to remain in Minnesota. We had a day of celebration. Silence was lifted!

This year of novitiate remains my most memorable encounter with God in prayer. It has been a formation of great value to me throughout my life. I personally owe my gratitude to Sister Henrita Osendorf, our novice mistress, so gifted at leading others into a life of prayer. Along with the essentially spiritual aspect came the training in everyday respect for others and for things. In Chapter 32 of his *Rule*, Saint Benedict reminds us to "regard all utensils and goods of the monastery as sacred vessels of the altar. . . ." Those practices which I automatically observe today are handling all things with respect, closing doors quietly, speaking in a modest tone of voice, avoiding loud, "show-off" behavior, and being genuine in character.

July 11, 1945, marked the day of first vows, and, three years later, in 1948, our class pronounced final vows, and we began our professional careers. No longer was there that sheltered, safe, and totally ordered day-by-day routine. Teaching in parish schools often left little time for balance between work and prayer. As years progressed, this conflict became more disturbing, adding to my fears and guilt; that which had been so important in formation was getting lost among all the activity and outside distraction. Frequently work became my prayer, not intended in Benedict's mind. We were put into the work world too suddenly without taking time for renewal of all the deeply spiritual jewels in Benedictine life. I was not able to submit to the idea of substituting action for time alone with God. Though it was often suggested to me, I rejected it in my heart, building up guilt.

My sister and I were assigned to do the type of work for which we were trained. Sister Rhoda and I, Sister Rhodene, were never to live together again because both were music teachers and each parish could use only one. We had always been supportive of each other, but suddenly that close tie ended. We had to do without each other. The sting of separation is still somewhat present in each of our lives today. I have been away from Saint Benedict's for thirty years, while she has remained in the monastery, and I am proud of her following her own life-style.

My profession in teaching brought a great deal of satisfaction and joy to my life as a sister. Music, choir work, classroom teaching, and private piano lessons filled my years from 1946 to 1964 in Melrose, Stillwater, White Earth, New Munich, Dumont, and St. Anthony's and St. Peter's parishes in St. Cloud.

The one place dearest to my heart was New Munich. I spent nine great years there, 1950 to 1959. Father Othmar Hohmann, O.S.B., was not only the resident pastor but also a drama director, using all local talent. He drew full-house crowds for every performance. He directed the acting and speaking parts, while I produced the music. A local artist painted all the scenery required for each play. The productions I recall are *The Song of Bernadette, Heidi, Hansel and Gretel* and a Christmas drama each year. These plays were hard work, professionally staged and fascinating.

The last parish in which I worked before leaving the monastery was St. Peter's in St. Cloud. Here I taught eighth grade and formed a boys' choir. Because of my training in both music and classroom teaching, both fields of work were always demanded of me.

Upon leaving the monastery in 1964, I spent several weeks in St. Mary's Hospital in Minneapolis. While there I experienced a deep sense of peace, being liberated from several years of fear and guilt, which I believe followed from years of struggling under many customs and rules that blocked the freedom for me to live out the principles of the *Rule*. Examples of misplaced emphasis included asking permission for every need—a pen, paper, a bar of soap, tooth brush—for each trip anywhere, even to visit a student in the home, or to make a telephone call. Much time was utilized in finding the right moment to see a superior for a small request. We also had a practice called "Culpa," in which we accused ourselves of little faults and failings as we knelt in front of everyone. Laboring over such trifles caused me to neglect the beautiful jewels of the *Rule*: the perfection of charity, holiness of life, seeking God in prayer, meditation, and Scripture. I felt the monastery was too much like the army, where many injunctions were placed on everyone, with little or no freedom of action, rather than a place where each person can follow Christ in an inner personal relationship.

Today, when I visit Saint Benedict's, I am pleased to find a sense of peacefulness and freedom that is most beautiful, and which certainly demonstrates a community of many members living for a single purpose but having true individual freedom of spirit. I think that monastics have regained their personal and communal identity through a deeper penetration of the spirit of the *Rule*, which now permeates their life-style according to the mind of Benedict. Gifts and talents are recognized and used to praise God.

After two years of adjustment to living alone and teaching school, things went well with me. I found time to pray about my future, whether or not I should return to the monastery. My greatest support, as always, in every step I made was my twin sister and our two Benedictine brothers. At the close of each day, I prayed before the statue of Saint Joseph in the parish church of St. Margaret Mary in Golden Valley, Minnesota, and begged Saint Joseph to guide my decision and to find a husband for me, if God willed it. That was the most visible answer I have ever had from prayer. Edward Roehrich came into my life most providentially, and I believed Saint Joseph had answered my pleas. I had already made my decision to remain outside the monastery where I had greater freedom to live out the spirit of the *Rule* wherever I might be. Ed and I were married at St. Anne's Church in Minneapolis on June 11, 1966. We moved to Bismarck, North Dakota, where Ed had purchased a house across the street from the Church of St. Anne. Here we did team work in many facets of church service, particularly in coordinating the Religious Education Program. On June 11, 1989, Ed was ordained to the permanent diaconate.

In 1969, I had one of my lifelong dreams come true: I became the mother of a baby girl, Susan Ann. She has been the most precious gift to us as parents. We are proud to have raised a loving daughter like Susan, whose faith has not diminished throughout her education as a lawyer.

Fran Hunkler Roehrich. Taken from a family photo, 1994.

After twenty-eight years of happy marriage I lost my husband Ed, in sudden death, July 25, 1994. Though his death was difficult for Susan and me to accept, it was a test of living by our spiritual values. Faith and trust in God must come before all else, even the security of a spouse and father.

In summary, I am extremely grateful to my family, especially to my convert mother, who formed me spiritually, to my friends in and out of the community, to my husband and my daughter, and above all, to my God. Saint Benedict's Monastery is still home to me. I personally would like to rejoin its ranks, if it were possible, but since that is a little out of reach, I will bear with that one unsatisfied desire. My days are full, life has been good, and I have a heart filled with gratitude.

Fran Hunkler Roehrich *lives in Bismarck, North Dakota. She continues to be active in her parish of St. Anne, where she is an organist and coordinates the religious education program. She is a volunteer organist and lector at Marillac Manor, an apartment complex associated with St. Vincent's Care Center.*

Chapter Two

Wind in the Pine Tree

EILEEN MAAS NALEVANKO

NEW YORK CITY, 1968. IT WAS SPRING, and the city was alive. A colleague and I were attending the National Conference of the Council of Diploma Programs in Nursing. During an afternoon break in the meetings, we went to our room in the Waldorf Astoria to lie down. Scapulars were removed and veils flipped above our heads to prevent wrinkles. I closed my eyes and tried to slow down my breathing, allowing my muscles to relax. After a short time, I was suddenly aware of a very deep inner peace and the words forming quietly in my mind: "I am going to leave the convent." That moment was the beginning of the end of my life as a religious. How did I come to that moment? And where did it lead me?

I had been born into a family of eight children, six girls and two boys: Bob, me, Dianne, Leon and LaVonne (twins), Marilyn, Arlys, and Bonnie. (LaVonne would follow me into the convent where she remains to this day). My parents, Louis and Lorraine Maas, were good, honest, hard-working people who struggled to support their growing family at a time when the Great Depression was wreaking havoc on millions of lives. As the two oldest, my brother Bob and I learned very early to be helpful around the house, caring for the younger ones and doing chores. Play time was a creative time. We always found something to do: checking all the gravestones in the Baptist Cemetery across the road, hide and seek, jacks, checkers, cards. We shared everything, including quarantines for measles, mumps, and chickenpox. We learned to enjoy little things and to share them selflessly. On very rare occasions my father brought home two Milky Way bars, which were cut into four pieces. How we savored that treat—I can taste it still.

Church and school formed the foundation of our lives. Sunday Mass was an absolute must, as were regular confession and communion. Our education took place in a four-room school under the direction of the Benedictines from St. Joseph. They were very influential in my life. From the beginning of my first grade until I graduated from eighth grade, the nuns frequently told me they thought some day I would be a nun. The wonder of it all was that I never questioned it. Since I loved and admired them and was also beloved of a tempestuous old German pastor, it never occurred to me that I should give it some serious thought. My main impulse was to please those I loved.

So it was that in 1943, at age thirteen, I left home to attend Saint Benedict's Academy as an aspirant. It was very hard to leave home, but I swallowed my tears and in due time overcame the homesickness. School was a joy for me. I had learned to love reading during the elementary school years, often stopping at the small library on the way home to exchange books. Now I was enjoying new experiences as I studied Latin, literature, and history. I learned to appreciate music through four years of college recitals, where attendance was required. Lasting friendships were formed.

Sister Leonelle Maas, 1963.

In June of 1947, at age seventeen, I graduated from the academy and became a novice, Sister Leonelle. While many aspects of the life in community became comfortable, I missed my family and felt uprooted. Toward the end of the year in the novitiate, my grandfather died. It was June, and Sister Henrita, our novice mistress, took me out to the porch. We sat there on a bench as she read to me only selected parts of the letter from my mother. I remember being stunned and not saying a word. I felt "disconnected" in some strange way.

After first vows I was sent to the Diocesan Teachers College in St. Paul to become an elementary school teacher. The prospect terrified me. While I enjoyed school, the idea of teaching little children didn't seem to fit me. As the senior students went to do their student teaching, I was even more sure I could never do this well. God must have had mercy on me. Just as I was preparing to leave Saint Benedict's for a second year in St. Paul, Mother Richarda asked to see me. I was dumbfounded when she said that she wanted me to try nursing. Since some nuns thought I would make a good nurse, I was to go to the St. Cloud Hospital and start at the School of Nursing. This news was a bit overwhelming; I was now nineteen years old and knew nothing about nursing. That change, for me, was an example of God writing straight with crooked lines. It was the stepping stone to a good career in nursing and eventually in nursing education.

Life in community, meanwhile, took on a kind of soothing regularity for me. The daily routines, while not always my choice, were such that I could pursue my career with full vigor while actively participating in community. My job assignments gave me ever-increasing responsibility. I felt wonderfully supported by the many sisters who lived with me. We grew to know each other well, to understand each other's needs, and to care about one another. Our recreation periods were fun—a walk with friends, playing cards, singing, playing volleyball with gusto, square dancing.

While I never particularly relished long periods of silence, I was always grateful for the quiet at the end of the day. I learned to love the quiet times and to enjoy periods of solitude. While long retreats were tedious for me, there was something about a large group of nuns in retreat that was rejuvenating. In addition to the spiritual benefits, the retreats provided time for solitary walks to the woods through the lane of spruce and pines. To this day, the soft sough of the wind in a pine tree takes me instantly to that path to the woods and fills me with peace— and some longing. I've always been thankful for the ability to be with myself in peace and quiet.

My professional career provided excellent experiences. I tried always to do my very best, something which at times cost me in the area of my own health. After about fifteen years as a staff nurse, head nurse, and director of nursing service at a small hospital, I was given an opportunity to complete my B.S. in nursing at Boston College. In 1964, I earned an M.S. in medical-surgical nursing at Boston College Graduate

School. When these studies were complete, I was assigned to be a coordinator on the faculty of the St. Cloud School of Nursing. After one year, Mother Henrita called on me to tell me I was to be director of the School of Nursing. My protest: I was prepared for education but not administration. This fell on deaf ears. She told me that I was the most prepared person available, and I would have to do it. After Mother Henrita left, I went to my small office, stared at the fish in my small aquarium, and cried my heart out. It was an example of a major concern, one I shared with Mother Henrita: the better one became at something, the sooner one would be promoted to something else. Staff nursing, being with patients, had been my first love, and I was slowly but surely being taken farther away from it. I now felt light years away from what I did best.

In 1964, about the time I returned from Boston, I began to experience an inner sadness, a kind of desolation which would not be appeased. The stress of it became severe enough that I spent several years under the care of a psychiatrist. These were agonizing years. I felt an almost constant anxiety. The aloneness of it made it a very gut-wrenching time. Certainly my friends were there for me, but I was never able to share my anguish. Although it was so pervasive, I couldn't identify the heart of it. Nights were often sleepless. Days were sometimes helpful in that I had a job to do, and that became an important part of my therapy. Prayer became difficult, if not impossible. It was obvious, I'm sure, that I was struggling, but in all that time only one of my fellow sisters caused me deliberate pain. As I passed the lunch room, she saw me go to the garage for a car to see the doctor. She said loudly: "There goes that nut case. She got an expensive education but what will we get back?" Perhaps I was supersensitive, but I never expected a fellow religious to attack me in such a vicious fashion. I was devastated.

During this time Sister LaVonne was living a few blocks from the hospital, and we often went for walks in the evening. Because it didn't seem right to burden her with my problems, I carefully chose what we discussed. Meanwhile, my friendship with a young couple in New Prague, Jean and Mike Rybak, probably provided the greatest tangible support during the painful years. Jean and I had worked together from 11:00 P.M. to 7:00 A.M. at Queen of Peace Hospital during my stay from 1955 to 1958. While I felt unwilling and in some sense unable to share my problems with my family and with my fellow religious, I was able to share some of my pain with Jean and Mike. Their love, concern, and continued support in everything I did gave me a great deal of comfort. They deserve my eternal gratitude. Jean and I are still close friends; Mike, sadly, died an untimely death of heart disease at age fifty-one.

Soon after returning from New York City, it was apparent to me that I must move on. I was convinced that while I could easily have lived on in community and enjoyed the security it offered, I could not live with the hypocrisy involved in doing so. Having explained all this to Mother Henrita and sharing some tearful moments with her, I wrote to Rome for the Indult of Exclaustration. From the time that letter was placed in the mail, every moment seemed like an eternity. I now began to grieve in earnest as I anticipated leaving the family and the life I had loved and still love. I lived with constant tears in my eyes and a huge lump in my throat. In spite of the profound pain, I knew my decision was right and had no regrets on that score. But the response from Rome seemed to take forever. When I finally could not bear any more pain, I called Mother Henrita and told her I needed to leave to retain some sanity; she encouraged me to do so. The Indult would come later. Meanwhile, I arranged with my father, then in his early sixties, to come for me. I carefully packed a small suitcase with only my personal, private things. When my father was announced a few days later, I took my little suitcase and quickly went to the car. It was to be the first day of the rest of my life.

One of the most painful aspects was the secret nature of my leaving. My parents knew, of course. Sister LaVonne, who had also recently learned of it, had gone home with me some weeks earlier to inform them of my decision. As far as I knew, no one else was aware of my leaving. I had never heard anyone discuss plans to leave with their fellow sisters, and I quietly assumed it would be inappropriate. This deprived me of the support I needed but also deprived my religious family of the chance to wish me well. It left me with a huge hole in my heart and caused intense grief. Because I was so steeped in my own pain, it never occurred to me that my fellow religious would also feel the pain of not being able to say good-bye and to deal with the failure they felt for having "let me down when I needed them." Many years would pass before this realization came to me.

So I began another chapter of my life. I spent two weeks with my parents, sleeping much of the time to ease my utter exhaustion. With my family's help, especially that of my mother, I took the $500 the community gave me, and purchased only the absolute essentials: a few clothes, a nursing uniform, toiletries. I went to several hospitals to apply for a job as a staff nurse in orthopedics. I hoped eventually to be an instructor of professional nursing students again. The director of nursing at Methodist Hospital in St. Louis Park hired me on the spot for the job I requested. Since salary scales did not allow for a master's degree, she offered me $700 a month—off the scale. I was in heaven, or so I thought. The third week I moved into my brother Bob's home in Hopkins for a month or so until I could earn enough to rent a furnished apartment. He helped me buy a new car and secure a loan to pay for it. Because the idea of debt was uncomfortable for me, I wanted to pay off the car in two years. That's how I arranged it, but without having received my first paycheck. That was an eye-opener. Never having seen an actual paycheck, I was unprepared for the total amount deducted for state and federal taxes and social security. I had now moved into a furnished apartment for $180 a month and had car payments to make. This left me with $15 a week to spend for all my needs—gas for the car, clothing, food, insurances, and recreation. While I had lived the spirit of poverty in the convent, I was now living the real thing. My background prepared me well for this. I had to go without many of the necessities. When winter came I could no longer put off buying a coat and boots. Mom kept her earnings from a cleaning job for the well-to-do in a pickle jar in her basement. Periodically she raided it for me, allowing me to pay it back as I could afford. And I did! The bank manager had also allowed me to refinance the car loan without charge. My very honest but humble explanation was all that was required.

There were many hurdles in those early days. Chief among them was the conviction that the words "I was a nun" were emblazoned on my forehead. I assumed everybody knew intuitively. That assumption was validated one day by the director of nursing. She told me that the dignified walk and precise grooming said there was something special about me, even to the people who did not know. It told me that while one could take the nun out of the convent, one couldn't take all of the convent out of the nun. Years later, the secretary in the college department where I taught nursing surprised me one day by telling me that no matter what happened there seemed to be something quiet and peaceful about me. Community life had helped me develop a solid inner core—a source of comfort and strength in troubled times.

After a year as a staff nurse, I took a new position, instructor in nursing, at the diploma school at Methodist Hospital. That position would last five years, after which the school would close. I accepted a similar position at North Hennepin Community College and held it for fifteen years. Those years of teaching were rich in opportunities to utilize my Benedictine values. They enabled me to reach out to the troubled, both students and the hospital patients to whom they ministered. Students and I often discussed the life-giving power of work, the fact that work well done could be one's prayer as we gave witness to the gifts we had been given. There were many lessons on the use and care of supplies and equipment, since, as Saint Benedict said, they were to be regarded "as sacred vessels of the altar." With the introduction of disposable supplies, waste due to carelessness became a serious problem that had to be addressed over and over. One of my roles was to help the nursing students achieve some degree of order and moderation in their hectic lives and to encourage them to take a few minutes to be quiet with themselves. I wanted very much for them to enjoy the journey to their RN license as much as the goal. Their reaction was utter amazement when I shared that I had always loved being a student and learning. It was my hope that they could also enjoy their work as nurses, instead of seeing it as a means to a paycheck and nothing more. The very heart of nursing is caring. Nursing would also be a joy to them if they could see their work as ministering graciously to those in need.

Not quite a year after I left the convent, I met the man I would marry. I met him as the result of an introduction by one of my patients. John Nalevanko was a widower of about four years, alone in caring for his eleven-year-old son, Gary. We married on December 27, 1969, when I was forty years old. Now I was new not only in my teaching career but also as a wife to John and a step-mother to Gary. None of us was prepared for our life together. Each of us suffered many times and for many reasons. Problems invariably found one of us standing alone. We enjoyed some good times, especially once I learned to cook a little. Somehow we endured the bad years, and now, these many years later, we are all the better for it. That inner core of tranquility became my salvation. I might be struggling in my marriage, but I knew I was a good person who gave everything I had. The stresses and strains, however, gradually wore me down, and eventually I had less energy for prayer and church. Survival seemed my top priority. For about seventeen years, I would be an occasional worshiper, never finding a real niche, a place where I could refresh my soul and also feel part of a vital community.

Through all those years, from June of 1947 onward, there was always an unidentified sense of aloneness, of a certain emptiness in my heart. Although I had been a member in good standing when I left my fellow religious, I felt unable to go to Saint Benedict's to see my friends and family. Several times I persuaded my husband to go with me. We parked at some distance and walked out to the cemetery. Many of my former colleagues were there by then. I knew I could visit them and talk to them, but the deep hurt never healed.

And then the letter came: an invitation to a renewal of friendships for all former members of the community. About eighty of us accepted, and in August of 1993 we spent a weekend with the community of women we had left. There was time for sharing, for praying, for crying, for saying the good-byes we had never said, for learning to appreciate the sadness of those we had left behind. Surely that weekend was for all of us a "defining moment" in our lives. The joyful welcome and embrace of all we had loved became the healing balm for our souls. It is impossible to describe the power, the intensity of the emotions as we were welcomed home so lovingly. By the end of the weekend I had shed copious tears, tears of sadness for what I had lost and tears of joy for what I had regained. There was no doubt in my mind. I was forever their sister.

In 1998, at the age of sixty-eight, I feel I have been abundantly blessed. I enjoy the love and friendship of my brothers and sisters, their spouses and families. I treasure the years I spent in the community. They helped in every way to define who I am. I've been married to John for twenty-eight years. My stepson, long grown, recently married a lovely woman, Anne, who brought an eight-year old daughter, Emily, with her to the marriage. They have also had a first child together, a beautiful little boy, Elias John. All of them give us great joy. A few years ago, John and I were able to purchase property on a lake twelve miles southwest of Saint Benedict's. We built a lovely home there with open space and lots of windows all around. Here John and I experience quiet and even solitude, which refresh the body and soul. We enjoy the seasons, observing especially the changes in nature, the birds and waterfowl, some of which come to stay near our feeders and others merely to visit on their annual migrations. We share the value of work and take pride in what we do. We live moderately and are reasonably healthy. We have friends who are caring and with whom we share a passion for fishing. We have family members who continue to love us and allow us to love them. Being near to Saint Benedict's allows me to be there frequently, visiting or helping in some small way to express my love and gratitude. Each time I go there I am surrounded by the warmth and gracious hospitality of my sisters in Christ. The pain, the sadness and despair of those earlier years are gone, allowing me to experience the people and the places I once knew with a heart full of love and gratitude.

Eileen Maas Nalevenko. Taken from a family photo, 1994. (Photo taken at Brinkman Studio)

Eileen Maas Nalevanko *and her husband, John, live on Grand Lake near Rockville, Minnesota. They enjoy the quiet, relaxed environment and often spend time fishing. Their son, Gary, and his family are frequent visitors, giving them a chance to enjoy their grandchildren.*

Quiet moments at the grotto, circa 1940s. (Courtesy of St. Benedict's Monastery archives)

Chapter Three

The Best of Two Worlds

Pat Roemer Gandolfo

LIFE BEGAN FOR ME ON NOVEMBER 5, 1928, slightly before the Great Depression. I was fifth in a line of six children: three boys and three girls. My parents were both of good German stock, blessed with strong characters and full of determination. My father, a convert to the Catholic faith, instilled in us a deep respect for everything connected to the Church and its teachings. He was a victim of polio, which left him handicapped at a very young age. Due to tuberculosis, my mother was in a weakened condition at the birth of my younger sister in January of 1930; she died two months later. My Aunt Sue took my newborn baby sister to raise, and, with the help of Aunt Pat, my father was able to keep the rest of us together as a family.

My educational life was completely Benedictine. From my first year of formal learning through two years of college, I was taught by Benedictines. Naturally this influence was very strong in my life. The sisters entered my life as teachers, counselors, disciplinarians, providers of food and, in one instance that I remember, as a seamstress for a new Easter dress for me. Indeed, it was Sister Ann, a Cathedral High School sociology teacher, who, at the request of my older sister, told me the "facts of life." All this left me with a warm and loving impression of these wonderful women of God and Saint Benedict.

The summer before my junior year at Cathedral High School, in 1944, my father passed away. I still had my junior and senior years to go.

16

Because I was the only child left at home, I had been taking care of my father. My older sister had married, and my brothers were all in military service. Now I was alone. However, Aunt Sue offered to let me live with her during my last years of high school. When graduation was approaching, I was not sure where to turn. I felt I could not remain dependent on my aunt; my older sister was raising a family of her own; and my brothers in service were at a great distance from me. Who should come to mind but the Benedictine community. In my younger years I had often thought of the possibility of becoming a nun. Now, with that stubborn German character I had inherited, I decided to go out to Saint Benedict's for an introduction. It was a vulnerable time for me to make a lifetime decision. When I was accepted, I was happy to be able to say I belonged someplace.

Postulancy and novitiate followed, and then, as a new junior sister, I was assigned to the Saint Cloud Hospital as my first mission. Because my typing skills were considered good, I was to assist in the Admitting Office and help at the information desk. I liked the urgency of life in a hospital, always much excitement, especially on night duty. We indulged in a few nighttime shenanigans now and then, playing tricks on Sister Melitta to repay her for playing tricks on us. Twelve-hour shifts got to be quite long at times and caused much drowsiness. I remember a particularly quiet night when admissions were very slow and time was dragging terribly. I tried to say my prayers, but every time I began reading, my eyes would droop, and I decided to lay my head on the switchboard for a few minutes. Wrong! It was getting close to 5:00 A.M., the wake-up time for the community to prepare for Lauds at 5:30; 5:00 came, no bell; 5:15 passed, no bell; 5:20 approached, and it must have been my guardian angel who finally got through to me. Awaking with a start, I quickly rang the wake-up bells and ten minutes later rang the bell to assemble in chapel. I peeked down the hall to observe the chaos I had caused among the ranks, and I didn't like what I saw. Nuns were running every which way with wonder on their faces and questioning glances at each other. As luck would have it, on my way to breakfast, I ran the gauntlet, meeting almost every member of the community, all of whom wanted to know what had happened. On entering the superior's office to confess my weakness and ask for a penance, I was asked, "How many nuns did you meet this morning?" I replied, "I think it was the whole community!" She said, "Well, Sister, you've had your penance. Go and get a good day's sleep. I don't think this will happen again very soon."

My time at the hospital ended after ten years. In 1958, I was assigned to help Sister Ivan at St. Joseph's Home, in the section for the retired nuns. Some in the community considered that to be comparable to Timbuktu, but I found it a gold mine of challenges, further growth for one who might some day be in the same condition as the ones for whom I cared. After a year with these lovely ladies, I was asked to try my hand at filling in for a first grade teacher in Eden Valley who was on sick leave. Obedient as I vowed to be, with no teacher's training in my background, and willing to try anything once, I said I would go, thinking the Lord would see me through anything He asked me to do. Not surprisingly, that is just what He did.

There were times when I felt I couldn't find my rightful place in the community. Twice in my convent life I discussed the possibility of changing course but was dissuaded by the phrase, "It's a temptation of the devil." *Now* I ask, couldn't these doubts also have been nudges from God to turn onto a different road?

I completed one year as a first-grade teacher, and then, half way through the second year, an S.O.S. went out from the Motherhouse that a volunteer was needed for our mission in Taiwan. The nurse in the orphanage, Sister Annelda, needed surgery; and someone was needed to fill in for her. In my younger years, I had had dreams of being a foreign missionary. Yes, I volunteered. The story of my life: "Fools rush in where angels fear to tread." Now this fool, armed only with the English language, good will, and the grace of God, in one month's time was on her way to Taiwan.

The experiences of my Taiwan years would require a book of their own. To put them into a nutshell: I lost thirteen pounds the first week adjusting to a new diet; had a sixteen-hour-day schedule with twenty-four hours on call; and very slowly learned Chinese from the children and the people around me. The first three months I did a lot of happy gesturing. Smiles go a long way even without the language. We have stories of typhoons, the experiences of measles, whooping cough, and mumps running through the orphanage for a whole year with no means of isolation because of close quarters; little Tony, a malnourished child who died of pneumonia in my arms as I was taking him to the hospital; our little "dust-pan baby," who was rescued from a dirt pile, thrown there because her twin had died and they thought she was going to die anyway; little Adele, saved from a life of prostitution due to the Chinese sisters' intervention. We learned to cope with rats, centipedes, cockroaches, and snakes—mere inconveniences in the light of the beautiful lives of the children who were there.

I have a particularly amusing memory. Taiwan was an island with no sanitation system, thus requiring us to boil all drinking water and cook any food we consumed. Because the American sisters longed to have a fresh salad now and then, we decided to plant our own garden with tomatoes, lettuce, and other fresh produce. We had an older woman who helped us with the cleaning, such as emptying potties and tidying the children's dorms. She was instructed to empty all potties in the children's bathroom. However, I observed her one day making her way—potties in hand—not to the bathroom, but to the utility room. She was emptying those potties in our sprinkling can and watering our garden with its contents. So much for a fresh salad. Needless to say, we were very unhappy as we saw our plans for salad evaporating into the Taiwan air. That mission experience lasted ten years with many challenges and God's grace, plus that German stubbornness to see me through.

After my six years of learning the language on my own, the prioress decided to send me to the language school on the island. It was there that I again looked into my true vocation and received counseling. After two long years of prayer, I made the decision to leave the community, return to the States, and take the uncertain step of starting a new life at middle age. This difficult decision brought me a wonderfully deep peace, and I knew it was right. It was in 1971 that I informed the prioress of my decision, wrote to Rome for my dispensation, and returned to the United States. On my return, I was told not to come to the motherhouse but to go to my sister's home in St. Cloud, since my leaving had not been announced to the community. Of course, thoughts of rejection entered my mind—after twenty-three years of service, I would not now be accepted at "home." I tried not to dwell on these thoughts or brood over them. God's grace entered in and warded off any bitterness that might have taken hold. From that day to this, I visited Saint Benedict's only once, for Mother Henrita's funeral. I have made it a point never to look back and dwell on the past; therefore, I have never had any desire to return to Saint Benedict's.

I borrowed from my hospital experience as a Benedictine to get my first job. Stepping into the strange world of business, I worked for three years at Mount Sinai Hospital as switchboard operator and information clerk. I then transferred to another company, where I entered the secretarial world. God placed in my path many good people who helped me gain more knowledge and acquire good promotions. I spent the next eighteen years with this company, retiring from a position of administrative assistant to the chairman of the board and the president.

Pat Roemer Gandolfo, 1990.

The example of my father and the *Rule* of St. Benedict—teachings on prayer, loving service, joy, humility, and respect for authority—had a strong influence in my life. As for specific Benedictine influence in my present life, the *Rule* is so closely attuned with the Gospel teachings that it is difficult to separate the two. Benedict advocates prayer, service to others, joy, humility and respect for authority, as does the Gospel. Prayer is a big part of my life. I serve others in our church community, as well as in the civic community, tempering this service with humility. I have tried to live close to God in the service of His people no matter where I have been. I have no regrets. What I have been in the past has shaped me into the person I am in the present, and when I look in the mirror in the morning, I am not too unhappy with the person that I see.

I am in love with God and with a wonderful husband who is a native of Argentina and a former Jesuit priest. He has always been a loving support for me in all my endeavors. We live a very frugal, no-frills life, but a very joyful one. All that happened in my life was meant to be.

Pat Roemer Gandolfo *and her husband, Tony, members of St. Joseph the Worker Parish in Maple Grove, Minnesota, are both active in church and community groups. Tony is a member of the pastoral council, is a Eucharistic minister, works with Habitat for Humanity, drives for "Meals on Wheels" bringing hot meals to shut-ins, and is a board member in their townhouse association, as well as the head of the architectural committee. Pat volunteers at St. Therese Home in New Hope as a word processor in the public relations department, is a Eucharistic minister and lector, and helps cook for funeral luncheons for the parish. She is a member and script typist for "Story Theater," a group of senior volunteers whose purpose is to encourage children to read books.*

Chapter Four

The Golden Thread

ROSEMARY WOLTER

EVERYTHING I HAVE EVER WRITTEN that was worth reading I wrote with my heart, and everything I have ever done that was worth doing I did following my heart. My journey into convent life and out of it was a journey of the heart. Once again I am asking my heart to journey through those experiences, to open again to those years of extreme emotional intensity and to choose areas of experience that cut channels so deep they continue to flow in my life in a valuable, useful, life-expanding way.

Having gone through so much therapy related to releasing the destructive effects of those seventeen years, my immediate response was, there is nothing I want to keep. Knowing that this was not wholly true, nor even possible, I refocused my sight from the bad pictures to the good ones and discovered richness, love, and self-forgiveness. My first picture was that of the many wonderful friends who are still in religious life, especially those who were part of the forty-two women who entered the novitiate with me in 1947, and my faithful friend, Sister Paula Revier, who continued to write to me even through the time I did not want to write back. Immediately I knew that my relationship with my sisters was the valuable experience that I never want to lose. Their abiding love is the channel cut so deep that it continues to flow into my present life. They are the bridge between what seems to me two very different lifetimes.

The prologue to my convent lifetime was my freshman year at the College of St. Benedict in 1945. Astonished at the strength and courage of

21

the teachers, who at that time were all nuns, I studied them like a lesson in humanistic spirituality. They were intelligent, clear-thinking women who knew who they were and what they were doing. Some joyous radiance was reflected in their lives that permitted them to be at once both human and spiritual beings. They really cared about us. They wanted us to be strong and intelligent, too. This is my memory of those sisters. They were giants of power to me. I will love them forever, and forever they will be in my heart. Of course I wanted to be one of them. "There is only one tragedy," I learned from Leon Bloy, "and that is not to be a saint." I wanted to be a saint. It seemed simple and easy. And so, at the start of the following school year, I crossed from college to convent.

Sister Judith Wolter, 1963.

That is the entrance story of my lifetime as a Benedictine sister. The exit story is painful to tell and wet with tears and heartache. This side of a four-hour mini-series I could not adequately explain the reality of a seventeen-year experience in a religious community.

After the year of novitiate ending in 1948, I attended college for a year, then started the three-year nursing program at the Saint Cloud Hospital, which was then owned and managed by the Benedictine community. I had been hospitalized for a skin problem earlier in the year and felt strongly drawn to caring for the sick. It resonated with who I was.

After graduation I was asked if I would be willing to enter the one-year training program for nurse anesthetists that had recently opened in the same hospital. I did not want to do this. I could have said no, but my definition of the vow of obedience did not include a "no" to anything my superior asked of me. Nor did I differentiate between a professional supervisor and the religious superior. My superior's voice was God's will for me, and God's will was the most important thing in my life. As far back as third grade I remember having long discussions with my friend, Rosemary Boyle Petters, on "What does God want us to do?" As a child I think I was often in the spirit world talking to my angel, to the flower spirits, and loving trees as personal friends. In sixth grade I spent Christmas vacation reading the entire volume of *Lives of the Saints for Children*, a gift from my priest uncle for all of us. No one read it but me. This call of the Spirit like a golden thread weaving through the labyrinth of my life is in my genes, and saying "no" was not in my vocabulary at that time. I began an eleven-year period where nightmare merged into twilight zone. Seven or eight of those years I only vaguely remember—no details, just a generic memory of where I was and what work I did.

I have thought a great deal about the 1952 version of myself, passing through incredulity, anger, guilt, grief, and self-forgiveness. At that time I was playing the victim and was not taking responsibility for myself. I was an inexperienced country girl that I have finally come to love. Admiration for her I have yet to achieve.

Finishing the nurse anesthetist program in 1953, I continued to work in the anesthesia department until 1963, when I asked to leave the convent. Sister Henrita Osendorf was prioress at the time. She offered me the chance to be at the motherhouse in St. Joseph, an opportunity to rest, sort out thoughts, feelings, and options before making a final decision. I welcomed the offer. In autumn of 1963 permission from Rome to leave the convent was granted.

Why did I leave? I could list various events, people, situations. One would be sleep-deprivation, though the syndrome had not yet been acknowledged or named. The anesthesia department had a small staff with a large surgery schedule, plus directing and staffing the anesthesia school and covering twenty-four-hour call seven days weekly for both emergency surgery and all births. Births at that time averaged seven daily. One never got through the night without at least one to two, sometimes three and four calls to the delivery room. At times there were only two people to cover call, which meant we were on call every other night without provision for daytime naps, though I unwillingly had a few during Mass and meditation. This night-time work combined with a long day of stressful work added up to burn-out, depression, and zero spiritual life.

But all this is description of events, not the reason I left. Had events been different would I still be there? No, and the reason is simple. I did not want to be there anymore. Are there really any other reasons? My Golden Thread led elsewhere. Certainly there were always enough clues.

Even when life was at its best, there was always a small, nagging inner voice saying, something isn't right, this isn't what I want to do, I shouldn't be here. At that time the inner voice did not have as good a reputation as it now has. It was the voice of the devil, not to be heeded. I thought that if I wasn't meant to be here, someone else would surely notice, and I would be told to leave. At that time I was not ready or able to take responsibility for my life and my decisions. As the voice got louder and more nagging, I tried to kill it with workaholism but only succeeded in killing my emotional life. I became this automaton pretending to be human.

At the bottom of the pit it seemed to me that I had three choices—leave, die, or go crazy—and now I knew the choice was mine and only mine.

I take responsibility for my life now. I don't believe in victims. I believe that everything in my life was necessary to bring me to the grace and blessedness of this present moment. I am grateful for all of it. I have forgiven myself. There is no one else to forgive.

When I left in 1963, knowing that I could not then understand what had happened and how my healing would come to me, I put the entire pot on the back burner, not even on low, and focused on how to live in this glorious, complex world of the expansive sixties as a single woman, aged thirty-seven, with the experiences and emotions of a nineteen-year-old country kid with nightmares.

Here I want to thank my friend, Sister Colman O'Connell, who came into all my nightmares like Beatrice to Dante, bringing her presence of light and hope. This she did for years. I know that a great deal of healing took place in those dreams of shadows and shades with Colman as my guide. Thank you, my friend.

The day of reckoning came in 1971 in California, the state of encounter where walls must crumble and all those inner demons must come out of their hidden corners to be examined and dissolved in the light of love and trust.

I had lost my faith on Beacon Hill in Boston during the summer of 1966. Actually, it was lost before I left the convent, but, not wanting to believe this, I kept it a secret from myself and mistook its shadow for reality. In San Francisco, searching without success for my Golden Thread, I explored Eastern religions, psychic paths, Quakers, New Age, pagan religion, and on and on. The city was well stocked with options, and I learned something from each of them. I remember the day I realized I could never belong to an organized religion again. I cried a lot. The daily bread that my being, my *self*, was looking for was the experience of humanism and mysticism blended in an unlimited place of expansion.

Mostly what I experienced and accomplished in San Francisco was marriage, three sons, and mothering, a profession I loved more than any other and still do, most of the time. Chris was born in 1970 and the twins, Ben and Tom, in 1972. The following year, we started gradually working our way north through Marin and Contra Costa counties, finally settling in Mendocina County in 1977, where I still live.

This brings me to another experience from my life as a Benedictine sister that I continue to value and from which I continue to draw. It is the process of living communally. The wisdom I learned there, that flowed from the dynamics of human interaction in a close community, was hard-earned but useful and lasting.

Most of my life I have lived in some variation of community life, starting with my birth into a family of nine children. During the married chapter of my life, there was always someone living with us, a young married couple with a small baby, a pregnant young woman who did not want to be with her parents, friends in transition. When we moved to northern California to eighty-six acres of hills, streams, fruit and nut trees, and several living quarters in various conditions of completeness, we became, out of need rather than conscious planning, a haven for burned-out refugees from city life who needed a place to heal from job stress, drugs, divorce, and various other sufferings. They stayed weeks, they stayed months. Some became permanent members of the community.

Rosemary Wolter, 1995. (Taken from a family photo)

During my single-parent scene back in a small town again, there were always children other than mine living with us, mostly boys. Often they were kids having troubles at home and needing a temporary safe space away from parents. My neighbor told me years later that she thought I was running a half-way house for boys.

I did not realize it at the time, but as I reflect on it now, I believe I was using skills and wisdom gleaned from the experiences of my convent days.

Now, thirty-two years later, I am still holding tight to my Golden Thread, which has taken me in and out of convent, marriage, and a kind of insanity, through tremendous growth and change to this 1997 version of who *I am*. It has brought me to this place of paradox and mystery, a place where questions are irrelevant, and absolutes are hard to name. And don't ask about my tomorrow, change being one of the absolutes along with the never-ending possibility of *more*.

Pierre Teilhard de Chardin has told us that we are not so much human having a Divine experience, as Divine having a human experience.

After thirty-five years of involvement in the nursing profession, I retired last year. I am a Certified Amanae Practitioner. This is a type of emotional-release bodywork that is both healing and transformational. It is the therapy most successful and complete for me because it bypasses the busy mind, working directly on the body, releasing those stuffed-in emotions that are locked in my body, holding me in bondage and keeping me from realizing my essential, creative self. Truly, I was over-stuffed with them, and, though I'm not finished with this work, I know I am on track and headed in the right direction, following my Golden Thread.

Once again with intent and purpose I find myself living with three and sometimes four supportive, strong, intelligent women, all of us intensely dedicated to transformation both personal and planetary. The circle of friends that surrounds us includes women and men from a variety of professions, experiences, and ages, all following their inner wisdom on their spiritual journey, ever-changing, ever-expanding and deepening in these exciting and powerful times.

When I go to Saint Benedict's to be with my sisters there, I feel a powerful love connection with them. I feel embraced, surrounded, nourished by their goodness and love. The format is different but the essence is the same. It seems to me their circle is a part of a grand, ever-growing circle common to us both. Perhaps this is the grand circle composed of women and men who know who they are, who live in a space of love, not fear, hold peace like a shining star, and understand their partnership with the earth. "There is nothing so wise as a circle," Rilke said. It has no beginning, no end, no limit to its expansion, and all positions are equally important since there is neither top nor bottom.

Rosemary Wolter lives in the small city of Ukiah in northern California. She is a retired registered nurse who continues her healing profession as a certified practitioner of Reiki and Amanae; the latter is an emotional-release therapy that affects both the physical and spiritual being. She is also an environmental activist who belongs to Earth First! and recently spent two weeks in jail for protesting the continuing logging of the Headwaters ancient redwood forest. She has three sons, whom she adores.

Chapter Five

Lord, Let Me Know

ANN CALHOUN HANSEN

I TURNED DOWN UNIVERSITY AVENUE, catching a glimpse of the sun setting over the bay. I had become accustomed to blotting out buildings that
could easily obstruct my view, looking beyond them into the depth of the
mysteries unfolding in my life. God had let me wander down many roads
in my never-ending quest to do his will.

It was 1946. I was a discontented teenager, out of high school,
leaving home, unable to adjust to the changes of war and its aftermath.
As my father embraced me at the bus station, he asked me to promise
him two things. One was that out of my first paycheck, I would send five
dollars to Father Flanagan at Boys Town; the other was that I would
receive the Eucharist every Sunday. Although he sensed that I was losing touch with the church, he believed I would honor any promise I
made to him.

It was a long trip from Bemidji, Minnesota, to Crawfordsville,
Indiana, where I would go through Western Union training. I was alone,
very much alone. The flood gates opened at the Bemidji bus depot, and
the tears and sobs stopped only when I realized I had to meet company
officials at my destination. Red-eyed and weary, I embarked on my short
Western Union career.

I did well at my training, graduating second in my class, and was
very pleased to receive my assignment in the Rochester, Minnesota,
office.

I loved Rochester, a lovely city, where I spent much of my time alone. My work hours gave me free mornings when I would go for long walks. It was then that I did my serious thinking. I had sent the five dollars to Father Flanagan as I had promised my father but had not been inside a church since leaving home almost a year before. One morning I turned in a direction I had not walked before. All at once, I found myself standing before a beautiful church. I hesitated. I wanted to leave, but I couldn't. Almost without effort I walked up the steps.

I knelt alone in the quiet of the church. I had been experiencing discontent with my life's lack of meaning. I made no connection between my aimless wandering and my inability to accept the mantle of the church. I had distanced myself as much as possible from the church to deal with the guilt of not keeping my second promise to my father. When I became aware that Mass was beginning, I decided to stay. Tears poured down my cheeks as I realized how lonely I had become in my isolation from God and my family. The emptiness of my life lay before me. Long after Mass, I knelt there, unable to move, until I felt a hand on my shoulder and heard the priest asking if he could help.

It was spring—the season I loved. I reveled in the newness of the season as I left the rectory. The flowers were more beautiful, the air was fresher, and the singing of the birds was sweeter than ever. I had found peace, but it would take months of searching before the discontent in my life would be resolved.

Each morning at Mass I prayed for guidance. I spent hours before the shrine of Mary, always coming up empty. One day early in July, as clear as God's call to Saul must have been, I saw how I had spurned grace at every turn and methodically suppressed his call. From early childhood I had admired the lives of the sisters who taught us at Saint Aloysius School in Little Falls. I had wanted to be like Sister Evelyn, Sister Valencia, Sister Eusebia, and dear Sister Lucina. I wanted to be one of them—to be like them. Now I knew why—they were close to God, and they were doing God's work. I knew that this was God's call and set about gaining entrance to Saint Benedict's Convent in Saint Joseph, Minnesota.

I loved Saint Benedict's, as I still do, from my first moment there. I did not visit beforehand, for I believed in my heart that I was destined to be there. The community was in transition as preparations were made for the founding of priories at St Paul and Eau Claire. After the novitiate

I was among those sent out unprepared for the responsibilities assigned. The vacancies created by the sisters going to the new priories had to be filled.

Sister Marmion Calhoun, 1947.

I was very willing to do everything I could for the community I loved. Undoubtedly I made the mistake of concentrating on the work part of the "Ora et Labora" motto, as I found myself in ever increasing degrees of responsibility. Each time I met the challenge with the same generosity but inexperienced, not trained or educated. Eventually feelings of inferiority took command. I could not see my successes; and my mind, darkened by failure, told me I had failed in my religious life and my contribution to the community. I experienced a complete break with reality through my desperate attempt to be part of the community.

God does not abandon his beloved. The guidance I received brought me full recovery and a belief in myself that has never again been shaken. With new confidence, I accepted the assignments I was given and felt sure I could succeed at whatever I was asked to do. I had become whole again, with a much stronger realization of my worth as a child of God. My religious life now had new meaning. The pivotal point of all I did was God and my relationship to him. I valued every opportunity to serve others, to bring them to him. All my work not only became a prayer but was possible because of the strength of my prayer life.

One problem remained. I was the least trained and least "qualified" for assignments I was given. Although there was no question of succeeding in my work, I began to realize it was difficult for others to accept my ideas. I was forward looking, and had I possessed that "piece of paper" so sought after, I might have been more accepted. Living and working with the same people, I found it difficult to erase barriers. I believed God wanted me to develop the potential he had given me, but I did not feel free to do so.

It was with difficulty that I realized I must leave the community. Even though I did not want this, once it became clear to me, after counseling, that my development as a person was at stake, I knew I must. The intensity of my prayer equaled, if not surpassed, the prayer that led me to Saint Benedict's, and, in 1968, I left.

It was an unceremonious departure with none of the splendor of reception and profession, but equally definitive. As I lay on the couch in my friend's apartment I pondered, "I don't have a bed of my own—I do not have a home." Yet I wasn't frightened; I knew I was doing the right thing.

I had chosen California for several reasons. I had never traveled. My position as number ten in the family had precluded many of the experiences of my siblings. When the war came, I went from being one of the youngest at home to being the oldest. Our family was scattered all over the world. I had not learned to drive until I was thirty-six years old since my father needed all his gas ration for his sales route. Three of my brothers now lived in California, and my youngest brother and his wife wrote to tell me I could stay with them and their seven children. I felt that if I were making a break it should be a complete one. So, never having driven on freeways, never having seen a mountain or an ocean, and never having been west of the Dakotas, I headed west in my 1968 Impala purchased with a loan from a friend. I had five dresses, three pair of shoes, a coat, a hat, a box of books, and two hundred dollars.

My brother's family welcomed me warmly, sharing their home, their friends, their life with me. My niece who lived south of San Francisco introduced me to the wonder of California—from Carmel to the astoundingly beautiful Yosemite National Park. She was a great companion and laughed hysterically when she treated me to fortune cookies and I swallowed my first fortune along with the cookie.

My teaching career in Berkeley began at the height of the unrest. It was the time of the hippies, free love, the SLA, People's Park riots, the Black Panthers and encounter groups. Women were beginning to feel their neglect, their frustration, and their power. The Church reflected the turmoil of modern thinking and the changes of Vatican II. In the years I lived in Berkeley, I worshiped at the Newman Center Holy Spirit Parish and directed the CCD program. I kept up on changes in this way, and my position served as a conduit for doing something for others.

I put my heart and my soul into teaching. Berkeley, always the seat of experimentation, was into many different projects. Multiple grades in one room, team teaching, master teacher for student teachers from UC Berkeley and San Francisco State—all of these were a part of my experience. I became involved in the teachers' organization and was staff representative on the Superintendent's Advisory Committee.

In recent years I had a chance meeting with a young man who had been my most serious problem child. We threw our arms around each other—so happy to see one another. He insisted that I should meet his boss. I was humbled and gratified as he told his boss that, if it had not been for my faith in him, he would never have finished school and would certainly be in jail. I had believed in him as a person, as a child of God, just as I had learned during those years at Saint Benedict's that I was a child of God and needed to develop into the person God wanted me to be.

I could tell many stories of successes and some failures. I was always cognizant of the fact that people looked to me for moral and ethical values. Often I encountered persons who had given up on the Church. There was Maria, who, because of a child born out of wedlock and a pastor's reaction to the situation, had separated herself from all her greatest values. After we became close friends, she asked if I could enroll her eight-year-old child in the CCD program at Holy Spirit Parish. I was delighted and arranged to pick her up each week to bring her to the center for instruction. Slowly attitudes changed, and the Church again took its place in her life. It was none too soon; she needed the spiritual strength when her daughter was killed in a car accident. At an early age Maria followed her daughter to eternal union with God.

As immersed as I was in my teaching and having close contact with my brothers and their families, I still felt an aloneness. I was always welcomed into the homes of my friends, and much as we shared our mutual love, I felt my relationships were not complete; there was no one with whom I could share myself completely. I did a great deal of soul searching about my life. Was I living a truly Christian life? Was it enough for me to dedicate myself to all the things I was doing? Did I need the relationship of marriage? Could I continue to live the single life? Did I want to do this? My conclusion was that I could but would rather dedicate myself to a person in marriage. However, I had not met the right person.

Living in the age of computers, I turned to that impersonal but objective instrument to find the person I wanted. I filled out lengthy questionnaires about my values, my likes, dislikes, and my spiritual inclinations, and mailed off my application. I met with psychologists and subjected myself to evaluations and waited for my "match." He did come, after some time, in the person of my dear husband, Lynn, with whom I have shared my life for twenty-six adventurous years. We were married February 27, 1971.

I was surprised that anyone could be as easy to live with as Lynn. We have encountered many difficulties but never any that threatened our relationship. There have been all of the trials of growing older, the death of parents and siblings, career changes, and necessary moves involved.

In 1973 we moved to Pinole, California, a community of about fifteen thousand people. We became involved in Saint Joseph's Parish, and, though Lynn had not yet joined the church, he was as involved as I was. During our time there, after making a Cursillo and being invited by the pastor, Lynn was received into the Church during Easter Vigil services.

While in Pinole, I kept busy teaching, working in our business, and participating in the activities of the business community. During a special election for city council, Lynn decided to enter the race because there was only one candidate; and Lynn didn't think he should go unchallenged. Lynn lost by twenty-nine votes—remarkable because we were little known in town.

Business owners, realizing that they had been shortsighted in not supporting Lynn, approached him asking him to run in the following election. He told them that he did not have time and they should ask me. Though I really wasn't at all sure I knew enough to fulfill the job, Lynn convinced me that I should do it. I campaigned hard and won. I was the top vote getter in a field of eight candidates for three seats and held a strong margin. I was only the second woman to be elected in the seventy-five-year history of the city. I was a bit bewildered by all the fuss; I simply saw a job to be done, and I was going to do it. In 1980, I became the first woman mayor of Pinole.

I resigned my teaching position in Berkeley in 1981. I looked around me and saw so many teachers who no longer had the spark, no longer sacrificed, who were waiting only for the magical retirement age. I realized that I could not let myself be one of them. Although it was too early for early retirement, I was sure that with my experience I would be able to get a job very easily. I was naive.

I was without a job for three years, finding that age discrimination was rampant. I went to a temporary agency and, upon fulfilling enough hours, was given cursory training in word processing. Then I went out on my first assignment to do credit reports. It was a breakthrough. Within a month the company hired me, and I subsequently worked my way up to credit analyst. I have completed eleven years as an analyst, five in my present position.

Although I no longer have the joy of working with children, I have been amazed at the great influence an attitude of prayer, respect, and love for others can have in a secular environment. We work in a fast-paced office, but there is always time to give a word of encouragement and offer prayers in distressing situations. Little by little the atmosphere becomes more God-centered.

Living in Benicia, California, I am happy to be a member of St. Dominic's Parish, which in the early years was the Motherhouse of the Western Division of the Dominican Order. It was the center from which priests went out to evangelize the area. We have been fortunate to have highly educated and zealous priests. We have celebrated the 100th year of the dedication of our church, which has withstood earthquakes and an infamous explosion at Port Chicago during World War II. I worked on the campaign that raised $800,000 in four weeks for seismic upgrading of the church and building a new parish hall.

There is a "coming home" feeling when I enter the church. The choir stalls and the great dome remind me of Saint Benedict's. I have known great joy in leading others to the Church by participation in the RCIA program and in reading the Word during the Eucharist. My years of table reading at Saint Benedict's prepared me well for being a lector.

Although Lynn and I have felt at home in Benicia, it may be that God's plan will take us to another place for our retirement. We are not sure where that might be, but to that end, we are making preparations by finishing up things we have started. I look forward to new challenges. Energy is ebbing a bit, but I know I will always find someone to help.

My main charity other than the Church is Habitat for Humanity. We recently built a house in five days. The thrill of seeing nothing but a slab at seven o'clock in the morning and within two hours the erection of four walls was overwhelming. There was great Christian solidarity as forty or fifty

Ann Calhoun Hansen, 1986.

33

men and women labored side by side to provide a home for a needy family. The volunteers were from all walks of life, and I greatly enjoyed the young lady who came each day wearing her sweatshirt that said, "Expect a miracle."

God has chosen all of us to work his miracles, miracles of love. I know that my ministry in life is love. The road I have traveled was always in answer to prayer.

Ann Calhoun Hansen *continues to live in Benicia, California. Her husband, Lynn, died on November 10, 1997. Ann is surrounded by young families, who affectionately refer to her as "Gramma Ann." While work and commuting take much of her time, she is active in her church as lector, Eucharistic minister, and Social Committee member. She is also publicity chair on the Solano County Habitat for Humanity Board of Directors.*

Community prayer in the Sacred Heart Chapel, circa 1940s. (Courtesy of St. Benedict's Monastery archives)

Chapter Six

My Life—Then and Now

Evelyn Ranweiler Crowley

I WAS BORN ON DECEMBER 1, 1934. My parents, Elizabeth and Louis Ranweiler, lived on a farm. I suppose we were considered "poor," although I didn't realize it; neither did the six other children. I thought we were rich in many ways. Both of my parents were devoutly Catholic, and I was decidedly influenced by them. We said grace before and after meals, recited the rosary each evening as a family, made the First Fridays and First Saturdays, attended Mass not only on Sundays but on every feast day. Religion played a key role in our home. How well I remember Father William Tarman, our parish priest, who had a personal library that included numerous young people's books on the lives of the saints. I came to know him and the saints by reading every one of his books, and I tried to emulate the saints and this saintly priest in those early years.

My faith, then, was very important and formed the framework of my early life. My very Catholic and strong-willed mother had a fervent wish to have one of her children go into the religious life or the priesthood. She inspired me to make her wish come true. It was this desire to please, especially to please my mother, that later caused me great difficulty in resolving problems centered on my religious life before being able to go on with my life outside of the convent.

Arriving at St. Benedict's in the fall of 1949, at the age of fourteen, I found myself faced with an utterly new and strange sort of life. The strict formation, together with the daily routine, times of silence and

35

prayer, cleaning duties and planned recreations I found difficult, but I genuinely tried to meet the challenges. In most respects I was able to comply. I was content with my life and all that I was asked to do. Oddly enough, while making friends got me into the most trouble in those early years of formation, I also learned to value the joys of friendship. I made special friends with sisters like Sister Eunice Antony, and I am delighted to say I still have friendships formed in those early high school days at St. Benedict's.

It was in my novitiate that questions related to "particular friendships" were resolved. The healthy and positive spirit with which my novice mistress, Sister Henrita Osendorf, encouraged me to love and enjoy others opened to me a world of trust and love. To this day I value this positive spirit, which she believed friendship to embody, and I am eternally grateful to her for her guidance. From Sister Henrita, I learned that Christian love is selfless, deep, and gentle but always centered in respect for others—believing in who other people are and acknowledging the priceless gift of their friendship. I still recall and marvel at what Sister Henrita so effortlessly opened to me—the door to true friendship.

After one year of college and the fall of my sophomore year, I was sent out on my first teaching assignment. This was a new challenge for me, but it was in teaching children that I discovered what I really loved to do. It was a joy to teach them religion, reading, 'riting and 'rithmetic—the four r's. The spirit of giving that the Sisters of St. Benedict instilled in me gave meaning to my teaching. I still try to keep this spirit with me today in my public school teaching, relying on my earlier knowledge and training to reach the minds and hearts of the little ones with whom I am entrusted.

As I was growing up on the farm, I learned a genuine concern and care for all living things from my parents. Later at St. Benedict's Convent, as Sister Jarlath, I came to reverence all things and to treat them as "vessels of the altar." It was at home, however, that I developed a tenderness for the small and helpless. I became a champion of the weak—which began a never-ending line of "adopted" pets, tame or wild. This devotion to God's creatures still engages me today, for my classroom never lacks little creatures (besides my first graders). It is a spirit of respect for all living things that I try to have the children experience. I hope they are helped to see how important and necessary is the care of all living things as they tend our rabbits, hamsters, tadpoles, fish, and various plants—or any other living thing that happens to be a "guest" in our classroom.

As previously mentioned, my mother had an ever growing influence on me. She dearly wanted me to become a nun, hoping to fulfill her perception of her unfulfilled life. My mother's resolve was much stronger than mine, for, each time I came home, she convinced me to return to the convent. However, even with the completion of my years of formation and later the profession of triennial vows, my doubts never ceased, but her determination never waned. In facing final vows, I had to weigh her respect, love, and hope for me against recurring doubts. I desperately wanted to please my mother and to fulfill her wish. On the day of my profession, I agonized sleeplessly into the night over the serious, life-long commitment I had made. I believed religious life was special— a chosen kind of life in which to serve God. As I cried on that evening back on July 11, 1957, I faced the fact that my motives were not coming to my rescue. However, I resolved that I would not give in to my feelings of despair but honor my vows. After all, I couldn't objectively conclude with certainty that I didn't have a religious vocation. For a time, this worked. My life was so busy in the service of others that I believed I could be happy. However, the feelings of frustration and rebellion against all the demands being placed on me stifled my spirit. In my immaturity, I handled these feelings of frustration and rebellion poorly, which in turn was followed by guilt—a recurring pattern of that part of my life. With the passage of time, the realization of how disappointed my mother would be if I left St. Benedict's, along with my own dwindling sense of self-worth, created a painful dilemma for me. In this confused state of mind, I struggled and agonized for years. Thankfully, I did receive the support and empathy of my fellow sisters.

In trying to conform to mission life, some of the unresolved conflicts of my earlier life started to bother me even more frequently. The resulting pressure of self-examination further defined a growing dissatisfaction in me. I am not sure that Vatican II had much to do with my eventual decision to leave the order; it just seemed to coincide within the time frame of what was happening to me in the convent context of my life. With the advice, support, and encouragement of close friends, especially Sister Emmanuel Renner, I sought professional help to see if I could come to terms with myself. I finally faced that I could have a worthwhile life outside of the convent, and that I was not going to ruin my mother's life by leaving. In the months of this decision the words of the popular female vocalist Petula Clark, "Go where I wanna go, do what I wanna do," from one of her hit songs became my own. Then, in the spring of 1968, with the consensus of all whose counsel I sought, I left the convent and moved to the city of Minneapolis feeling very unsure of just what my future outside of the convent might bring.

In the fall of 1969, I secured a teaching position in the Minneapolis Public School System after trying out a couple of different non-teaching types of work. During this time I developed a relationship with my future husband, John Crowley, marrying him in September 1971. Because of his former background as a Christian Brother, we had a common bond of understanding and shared much in the way of our Catholic beliefs and Christian faith. We have continued to grow in love and appreciation of each other these past twenty-five years.

Now, in the daily setting of teaching children, I feel that I am able to share the beautifully rich Benedictine heritage I lived those twenty years. A recurring thought within me is that little children need to have someone to help build trust in their lives by believing in them and treating them in a Christian manner. In my experience, children come to school to learn, to be accepted, and to have someone care for and about them. Besides teaching the children, I try to meet their other needs as well, often supplying them with field-trip expenses, school supplies, clothing—with whatever is necessary to improve their self-esteem as part of the class. While they might steal, use bad language, refuse to cooperate, and be anything but "model" students, they are still reaching out for acceptance in this "testing." At these times, I

Evelyn Ranweiler Crowley, 1997.

draw from the wealth of my experience in practicing Benedictine ideals, and I continue to use them in my secular life. In my opinion, my life as a Benedictine nun was nurturing to my becoming the very best teacher and human being I could in the world outside the convent.

Furthermore, I try to be a stabilizing influence in my students' lives by being there for them as they grow through the school year—reassuring them along the way to do what is right, although it may not be the easiest way. In keeping the spirit of the Benedictine rule of moderation, I try to provide for my students' diversity of needs by recognizing their individual differences. I also encourage them to respect one another and to treat one another well—and when they fail, to try again. While they need to value and respect themselves and others, and their material belongings, as learned in the care of things, they also need to learn to care for the world around them. The Christian treatment of each other is a priority of mine in interacting with children. I try to help them to extend this behavior to the adults in their lives as well. I hope the bond of mutual respect that develops between each child and me is a growing experience for both of us. Our friendship, born of trust, respect, and caring, is the basis of much that I hope to accomplish in working with children.

Early each morning as my day begins, I welcome a time of quiet and silence—a time of preparation to meet the challenges of the day ahead. I am thankful for the beautiful solace of these moments and the many years at St. Benedict's when I learned to cherish this part of the day. This quiet time of recollection and spiritual reading is very valuable to me even though I am no longer a nun. As I prepare for work, I use this quiet entry to the day as my *ora* before *labora* (prayer before work).

So, each day in my dealings with my husband, family, friends, colleagues, students, parents, and others, I believe a reflection of my past Benedictine life shines through. Each day has its demands and its rewards—joy and sadness along with success and failure claim a share of it. Strangely enough, it was in leaving the Sisters of St. Benedict that I realized how much the Rule of St. Benedict was to be a significant part of my life. I am still observing it these many years since being a member of the community. I lived a part of my life as a Benedictine nun, and, in spite of my earlier consternations about the life, I do not regret those years of spiritual and intellectual growth. I do not know that I am a result of Vatican II, but I do know that I am a product of Benedictine values!

39

Evelyn Ranweiler Crowley *continues to teach first grade in the Minneapolis Public School System where her husband, John, continues to teach biology at a local community college. Lynn and John both care for his ninety-year-old mother who lives with them along with their two Persian cats. Lynn and John are members of Corpus Christi Catholic Church near their home in Roseville.*

Monument in the monastery cemetery. (Courtesy of St. Benedict's Monastery archives)

Chapter Seven

I Will Plunge with My Song

Laurel Schneider Enneking

GERTRUDE VON LEFORT, IN HER BEAUTIFUL *Te Deum*, sings, "I will plunge with my song into the sea of Thy glory." This thought has been the inspiration for my life. I believe life is a melody to be lived, enhanced by people and events that touch us. As my life evolves, so does the fullness of my song. Come, plunge with my song.

Born in the spring of 1935, I was fifth in the Schneider family of nine girls and eight boys. I was named Laurel Ruth, after a special school friend of my mother. I enjoyed the challenges and opportunities of growing up on a farm near Breckenridge, Minnesota. Living with so many brothers and sisters was natural to me. There was always someone with whom to work and play.

Since toys were scarce, we invented our own kind of fun. Swinging Tarzan-style on the hayropes in the hay-mow, jumping from grain bin rafters into the golden grain, curling up in tires and rolling down the hill were a few of the creative adventures of farm life.

As for work, it seemed there was always more to do. Mom and Dad taught us to care for others and to be responsible for our share of the work. Through example and assistance, they instilled in us the importance of education and industriousness. Since we did not have electricity or indoor plumbing, we each graduated from one chore to another— pumping and carrying water, chopping and hauling wood, washing and hanging out wash, scraping and emptying ashes. Early in life, I learned about the harmony of working together.

With twelve younger brothers and sisters, I experienced a kind of mothering early in life. Dolls never seemed to make much sense to me since I played with and cared for the real thing. Needless to say, all those dirty diapers were not the best of the bargain. However, the generous hugs and kisses of each little one were ample reward.

During these growing-up years, there were many nights when we stood anxiously at the window, waiting, yet dreading, Daddy's late arrival home from town. We knew he would be drunk, and frightening things would happen. It was awful to hear him carrying on. We worried about Mom. We worried about each other. When he was not drinking, Daddy was a wonderful, caring father, but seeing this gentle side of him was the exception. I thought, "If only we were good enough, maybe he wouldn't drink." If I overheard Daddy or Mom wishing the garden weeded, potato bugs picked, or yard cleaned, I would rise early the next day to try to surprise them.

While scrubbing the floor one day, I heard my dad say, "With all our girls, we should have at least one sister in the family." "I'll be a sister, Daddy," I announced, not really knowing what a sister was, but knowing I would like very much to please my dad. From the time I announced that I would be a sister, my dad would proudly inform relatives and friends of this aspiration. When I graduated from eighth grade in 1949, it was assumed that I was going to Saint Benedict's Convent in St. Joseph. I would follow in the footsteps of Dad's sister, Sister Benezet. Admittedly, I had very little knowledge of what this entailed. I knew it must be something special, and I was confident that by my doing so Dad would be healed.

Entering the convent as a high school aspirant was truly an adventurous move. Activities were formative and memorable. Though shy and rather uncertain, I learned to appreciate opportunities for prayer and work. I adapted well to the rhythm of monastic life. Of course, I did find time for fun. Because I loved to read, after "lights out" I would sneak into the bathtub area and read by the light of the outside night light. Upon hearing the steps of the supervisor, I would hold my breath, lest I be caught.

On June 17, 1953, I became a novice and received the name Sister Bibiana. My religious formation was continued in the novitiate through the excellent guidance of Sister Henrita Osendorf. The Prologue to the *Holy Rule* of Saint Benedict encourages us: ". . . today if you hear His voice, harden not your heart . . . with faith and good works, let us walk in His paths by the guidance of the Gospel." I resolved to follow St. Benedict's admonitions for the rest of my life, pursuing perfection with all my heart. Often, as the moon warmed the cloister walk with its shadowy presence, I would steal away to the beautiful Sacred Heart Chapel. There I would kneel before the carrara Madonna, grateful for God's call to serve him and praying fervently for the healing that my daddy needed so badly. The flickering of the sanctuary lamp added a presence that assured me God was listening.

Novitiate year was a time of opportunities and a new beginning. Making coifs was a distinct challenge; packaging and shipping hosts to neighboring churches imbued me with a sense of responsibility; carrying the large cross while leading the funeral processions for our sisters was a humbling experience; summoning the courage to take my turn at intoning and chanting psalms and readings at Divine Office provided positive and rewarding feelings. These and many other experiences enriched the melody of my life that was emerging, measure by measure.

Sister Bibiana Schneider.

My mothering days as a child prepared me well for many satisfying years as a teacher and principal. During the summers, I earned my bachelor's degree from the College of Saint Benedict in St. Joseph, Minnesota, and my master's degree in education administration from Creighton University in Omaha, Nebraska. I loved it all. My simple melody was enhanced with new chords of enrichment.

In November 1974 my song hit a rather sour note. At least, I thought so at the time. Upon awakening from a breast biopsy, I realized I had had a radical mastectomy. I had cancer. I was only thirty-nine years old! I was devastated. Here I was, probably dying, and there was so much of life I had not experienced. I had never been on my own. I made up my mind that if I lived, I was going to do more with my life. I wasn't at all sure what I meant by that; I had no conscious thoughts of leaving Saint Benedict's at that time.

43

Upon recovering from surgery, I returned to teaching at St. Peter's School in St. Cloud. I loved teaching and felt a renewed dedication to that apostolate. Sister Dorothy Manuel, the principal, and the other sisters stationed at St. Peter's Convent provided the harmony that my song needed at that point in my life. We had beautifully enriching liturgies, memorable celebrations, fun, and a caring spirit. Yet I experienced a restlessness. I felt inadequate in my search for perfection. Trying to please so many people who touched my daily life became more and more frustrating. For twenty-eight years I had enjoyed the treasures of each new day, knowing that in all things I was doing my best. However, deep within, I was beginning to realize that being a people pleaser while living closely with so many people was destroying me.

Suddenly, on Memorial Day of 1977, I knew. I must leave my Benedictine community. God had another form of dedication planned for me, which I would incorporate into a broadening of opportunities for service. Maybe, subconsciously, I realized that I had done what I could for Daddy, who died in 1976; now I must be prepared to serve God along new and unchartered paths. Saint Benedict's Rule was again an inspiration to me: "Let your heart take courage and wait for the Lord." (Chapter 7)

Leaving my Benedictine family was a difficult decision. It was frightening to leave the security and comfort of my Benedictine community. In this decision, there was no one who could tell me what to do. Where would I go? What would I do? Could I get a job? Who would stand by me? In a very real sense, I felt as if I was losing my identity. My name would be gone; I would be lost to many friends and students who knew and loved me. I was leaving my cherished participation in beautiful liturgies and the Divine Office. I was stepping out into the foreign world of competition, taxes, and finding my own way in life, but my strong faith in God's presence strengthened and guided me. I felt sure that I was hearing God's call again. Having received a dispensation from Rome, I felt secure in God's continued guidance along this journey.

In July 1977, I realized that it was up to me to find a job soon. It was getting late in the season to find a teaching job. I called the Archdiocesan Office in St. Paul, hoping to find an opening. The principal of St. Alphonsus School in Brooklyn Center was there at that moment, looking for a second grade teacher. What a blessing! Most of my previous teaching experience had been in second grade. She invited me for an interview the next day. Not knowing much about big city driving nor the directions to Brooklyn Center, I called Reuben Muske, the college bus driver at Saint Benedict's for advice. Later that night Reuben and his wife Bernice called to offer to take me to St. Alphonsus. After a very favorable interview, the principal suggested that I look for an apartment nearby. Reuben and Bernice helped me find one only a few blocks away from the school. So, on August 5, 1977, with the help of very dear friends, I moved into my own apartment. What a relief it was to know that I could continue to do what I loved—teach!

During my second year at St. Alphonsus, a woman named Rose joined our staff. As we were going to school one day she said, "I know this really nice man. Would you like me to give him your telephone number? He's too old for me." I hesitated, but I was hoping to find someone who shared my values. I said, "Yes."

Very quickly we realized that we were a special gift to each other. Tom had been a dedicated Crosier brother for about twenty years. In June 1978 he had applied to Rome for a dispensation from his vows. Experiences in religious life had nurtured our common values and a special awareness of God's presence and guidance. We both had dedicated our lives to listening to and following God's will.

I had immediately sensed that Tom was that very special someone with whom I felt trust, peace, and a completeness of my person. Together we would accomplish great things for each other and for Christ. We were married at St. Alphonsus' Church on August 3, 1979. Our special dedication was to support each other so as to continue to grow in completing the "good work God had begun" as stated in the Rule of St. Benedict. A special gift at our marriage was the love and support of our families, religious communities, and friends.

By the middle of August, we had moved to Fremont, Nebraska, where Tom had been offered a supervisory job in a new 3M plant, and were happily settled in our little home on Parkview Drive. We became active members of St. Patrick's Church as lectors, Eucharistic ministers, CCD teachers. We were participants in organizing retreats, marriage support panels, and many other parish and community endeavors. Our successful experiences in our religious communities had prepared us well to extend our capabilities within this community. One very special opportunity was that of composing and delivering a homily for Valentine's Day in 1993. The theme was "it is not so much who you are or what you have that brings happiness and fulfillment in life, but who you have beside you along the way." I felt very blessed having my dear Thomas beside me. He is surely the one person I love to please.

In November 1979, I accepted a first grade teaching position at Clarkson School in Fremont. Teaching in a public school system was a new and rewarding experience. I found myself among very dedicated and talented educators. Because of my many prior opportunities, I was able to bring confidence, dedication, experience, and leadership into this educational program.

In my religious community, I had learned the joy that comes through loving acceptance of everyone. My love of children and teaching continued to enrich our personal lives with successful challenges and opportunities. During the ten years of teaching in Fremont, I taught all of the elementary grades except kindergarten and third. In 1985, I taught

School photo of Laurel Schneider Enneking.

a summer session graduate course, "Early Childhood Education," at Creighton University in Omaha, Nebraska. Through all of these teaching activities, Tom was there as helper and support. In return, I would visit him at break time when he had to work night shifts and weekends. Our intertwined lives enabled us to accomplish great things together. My life blossomed anew as I experienced the joy that comes in loving and pleasing one very special person.

During the course of the sixteen years we were at Fremont, my mother, two sisters, and a brother also moved to Fremont. Family support has always been important in our lives. We did what we could for each other to help make our lives happier and more comfortable. It was wonderful to have family nearby. Having Mom so close was a special blessing. I had left home when I was very young; now I had some choice time with her as an adult.

In 1990, Tom and I took over guardianship of my physically and mentally challenged sister, Nita. Though Nita continued to live with Mother, we did everything we could to ease and enrich their lives.

After ten years in Fremont, Mother expressed the desire to return to Minnesota to be near more of the family and the area where we had all grown up. This led us to evaluate our long-range goals. We decided that if Mother moved back to Minnesota, it would be wise for Nita to be close to her. That would necessitate our moving also. Why not? Since several failed back surgeries prevented me from teaching and since Tom had recently retired, we, too, were free to relocate.

On October 20, 1995, we put our house up for sale, praying earnestly that God would guide us in this move. We dearly loved our home in Fremont and have very special friends and ties there. However, Tom and I felt that, again, we were being challenged to "Listen. . . run while you have the light of life. . . ." (Prologue of Rule of Benedict). These past sixteen years together in Fremont had given the peace and happiness for which we had yearned. Now we were about to begin a whole new chorus of adventures. After sharing, listening, discerning, and praying, we decided to move to Avon, Minnesota, chosen for its proximity to St. Cloud, where Mother was to live, and near Melrose, where Tom had grown up. We would also be near many communities where I had taught, near many family members and friends.

Preparing to move took a lot of planning and coordination, but, with the help of family and friends, we were ready to move on October 30. At 10:00 that morning, we had the closing of the sale of our house in Fremont.

Immediately, we headed for Avon, amidst snow and looming excitement toward the unknown. Trusting that we were again following God's will, we confidently forged ahead. After an eleven-hour trip we arrived in Avon late that night, tired but excited.

On October 31, the next day, we had the closing of our new home in Avon. Though our furniture had not arrived, we slept in our new home, using sleeping bags and foam rubber. We met some of our new neighbors, who came "trick and treating."

My sister, Nita, lives with us here in Avon. Since she had her own apartment in Fremont, she will live with us only until we find something appropriate to her needs. She is a very responsible person and goes to work at Wacosa, a sheltered workshop in Waite Park, each weekday. We enjoy her presence and that of her kitty as well.

Avon is a small community, and we have been warmly welcomed. Being close to family and friends has enriched our lives. Though we miss our friends in Fremont, it is wonderful to be home in Minnesota. We feel truly blessed as we begin anew and plunge with our songs, into the sea of God's Glory.

Laurel Schneider Enneking's *song continues to resonate as she thrives in Avon with her loving husband, Thomas. Her sister, Anita, moved into her own apartment in November 1997 where she succeeds well with some continued assistance. Laurel is on the parish council. Both she and Tom assist St. Benedict's Parish and the thriving town of Avon in many ways. Playing cards—pinochle, five hundred, and bridge—with family, friends, and the elderly helps them keep their wits sharpened and provides social entertainment. They deliver Meals on Wheels for the needy in the area. Laurel relishes her past, cherishes the present, and welcomes the surprises of each new day. Life's adventures have provided a harmonious symphony for their lives.*

Chapter Eight

Other Orders

ANGIE TOUGAS PIHLMAN

FROM THE TIME I WAS EIGHT YEARS OLD, I said I would someday become a nun and teach ballet. The nun and teaching parts came true.

My parents, Hilma and Meddy Tougas, instilled in their six children a deep love for the Church and a strong sense of right and wrong. In Pelican Rapids, a predominantly Lutheran town in northwestern Minnesota, Catholics were a small minority. Although I probably imagined it, I felt a general prejudice against us.

My parents' pride in our "one true Church" made me strong. On Holy Days of Obligation, when I left school to attend Mass, I walked out of class with the courageous, though self-conscious, air of an Early Christian.

Benedictine nuns came to Pelican Rapids to teach catechism for two weeks every summer. I idolized them. I took their names when I played house and even named my dolls after them. The nuns epitomized wisdom, purity, kindness, and every other virtue I admired.

In February 1952, soon after my fifteenth birthday, Dad and I took donated children's clothing to the nuns at the While Earth Indian School north of our town. Sister Stanley, a friendly young nun, showed me around the boarding school. She was exuberant, describing her years of teaching needy children in the poor mission convent. I thought, how heroic she is to be happy in such a cold, dingy place.

Sister Stanley introduced me to the superior, who, upon learning that I wanted to become a nun, invited me into her dim, mysterious

49

office. She talked to me about my vocation. I liked her soft, gentle voice and the way she looked deeply into my eyes. She seemed so holy.

A few weeks later I told my parents I wanted to join the convent as soon as I could. My mother said if I truly had a calling from God, she did not want to stand in my way. But a few days later, I heard her tell my dad, "Angie's leaving home makes me cold all over."

During the next months, I worked out a plan. I rode the Greyhound bus to St. Benedict's, 125 miles from home, to see what the convent was really like. The aspirants in summer school made me feel so welcome I promised to return.

Bravely, my mother helped me pack a trunk with a few necessary things: towels and underclothes, a mirror and some curlers, school notebooks, a warm winter coat, and overshoes. Wisely, we added a stack of nice, ironed handkerchiefs.

Mother and I cried together, promising to write often. At times, I nearly changed my mind about dedicating myself to God. Then I'd think of how good it felt to know my life's work was finally decided and would soon begin.

At the end of summer my parents took me to the convent, where I became a uniformed aspirant and a junior in high school. Years later my mother would recall that ride: as I slept between them, she was overcome with fear, as though they were taking their sacrificial lamb to the slaughter.

During those first weeks, I often retreated to my dormitory alcove to reread my letters from home. Mother sent news of my four older brothers and their growing families. She told about my younger sister Bonnie, about Dad's latest wiring jobs, and what relatives had come to visit. I pictured everything they were doing, and I cried. Only the certainty that God had called me kept me from going back to them.

As the months passed, my concern became the pursuit of perfection. It puzzled me that some of my peers took liberties with the rules by violating silence, spitting down the stairwell, or roaming the halls after the 9:00 P.M. curfew. After all, I reasoned, we were studying to be nuns, so we should be perfect in everything we did. My own world was either white or black, right or wrong.

After my graduation, when barely seventeen, I became Sister Jennifer. Homesickness stayed with me during the year-long novitiate. I struggled to sublimate my longing by patterning myself after the nuns I had met in my early years. Sister Henrita, our novice mistress, recognizing my intense nature and desire to please, cautioned me to strive for perfection with an easier mind, since God was not a rigid taskmaster.

Still, it was difficult for me to justify straying into gray areas even when the rules didn't make sense. For instance, although I occasionally saw others doing it, I never allowed myself to set foot in someone's home, even as a courtesy, because our rules forbade it. That rigorous self-monitoring continued for most of the ten years I lived in vows.

Sister Jennifer Tougas.

One particular episode shook the resources of my zeal. That school-day morning I had delivered my class to Mass and then hurried to the convent to do my cleaning charge, not having any other time to do it. The superior found me at work and began an angry tirade about absenting myself from Mass where I was supposed to be. I felt shamed, like a bad child. Her distrust left me powerless and humiliated.

After a few similar experiences, I gradually settled into a pragmatic existence. When adherence to the straight-and-narrow meant going against my better judgment, but deviation into a gray area brought reprimand, I retreated into my private world peppered with resentment and frustration—and shrouded always in loneliness.

Along with that continuing sense of loneliness, a desire to expand the sphere of influence for nuns began to engulf me during the early 1960s. Pope John XXIII and the bishops of the world who gathered in Rome for the Second Vatican Council inspired me with new fervor. I envisioned dozens of ways we could break out of our mold and go to the people.

When two pupils from our school died in a tragic accident, I begged the superior to let us go to their homes on the funeral day to help with the other children. She refused, saying, "We don't do those things." Repressed and discouraged, I could not understand why the time was not ripe for our religious community to reach out, as I knew some other communities were doing.

Another issue became central in my life: I needed intimacy. In spite of being taught that particular, exclusive friendships disrupted community living, I eventually developed close friendships with some sisters. It felt good to be considered special by another person. I felt validated, worthwhile, warm and expansive. Daily life became a joy, and my energy soared.

But something was missing. It became clear, toward the end of my tenth year, that I was lonely not only for my home and family but for an intimate relationship with some*one*. To obtain that, I needed to leave the convent.

The thought of leaving caused me great inner turmoil, for I loved being a Bride of Christ and had always considered myself a "good nun." I asked for and received a professional psychological evaluation, and after a number of sessions, the doctor agreed I probably should leave. With a heavy heart and many tears, I saw my convent dream come to an end.

Through the years, my parents' anguish over our separation had changed to joy at my apparent happiness. They were exceedingly proud of their nun-daughter, so my next worry was the effect my leaving would have on them. After their initial shock, they surprised me when they did not crumble. Unselfishly, they supported my decision to start my new life in Seattle, where my brother and sister were living. Once again I said good-bye, boarded the train, and left home. It was October 1965.

Those next months were fascinating for all of us. In some ways my emotional life had stood still from the time I entered the convent, and I was seventeen all over again. I changed perceptibly, passing through stages of adjustment and awareness in my new world.

My first job was being a receptionist-secretary for five salesmen in a large truck manufacturing company. It was a far cry from teaching eighth graders in a small parochial school. I was self-conscious, hoping no one in the office could detect I had been a nun. My own reflection often startled me as I passed the big factory windows—my curled hair and pretty clothes.

If I needed a dress for a date, my sister Bonnie would sew one for me and then style my hair and apply my make-up. Her little daughters playing dress-up with high-heeled shoes and long gowns were not much different from their Auntie Angie.

Just six months after I left the convent, a friend introduced me to Ron Pihlman. From the start, each of us knew the other one was special. Ron responded to my resourcefulness and spontaneity, and I found his gentle ruggedness irresistible. That he was a quadriplegic from a car accident two years earlier meant our life together would be challenging, but we decided we were up to it. We married in 1967.

Ron and I led active lives, traveling, fishing, camping, and entertaining friends. We liked to invent ways to compensate for Ron's disabilities and capitalize on his strengths. Ron taught me to lay brick and finish cement, to tar a roof and build a wall. At those times I became his arms and legs.

Ron established an insurance agency, and, with help from friends, we converted an old gas station into his office. Later, we bought a house across the street. By installing an elevator, we found greater independence, for Ron could come and go from home without my help.

My love of academia, developed at St. Benedict's, led me to find employment at the University of Washington, where I worked for various professors over the years.

In 1977, we were blessed with the birth of a nephew, Aaron, to whom we became emotionally bonded. Ron and I had become resigned to being childless, but Aaron brought us joy beyond anything we had ever imagined.

My parents remained close to us, and we visited often over the years. Occasionally, when I'd do something my mother considered exceptional, she'd tell me, "Oh, dearie, I can tell you were a nun."

Married life gave me much opportunity to practice the virtues instilled in me by my parents and by St. Benedict's: people are more important than things, but things, too, should be treated with care; people in close quarters, like pennies rubbing against each other, can become polished and bright; there is a time for silence and a time to speak; labor of every kind is honorable. Ron came to quote St. Benedict's motto: "Do all things in moderation," as a guideline for business decisions. These truisms were part of our life together for twenty years.

Then, in early 1986, grief became my new companion. Ron developed terminal cancer. That May, Mother died suddenly from cancer. Nine months later, in February 1987, Dad had a fatal heart attack. When Ron finally died in April, at age forty-five, my world fell apart.

With loving support from family members and close friends, I maintained my courage. Time with friends from the convent proved life-giving, reminding me we were still sisters. With time, my inner peace returned.

In 1992, after twenty-three years at the University of Washington, I took early retirement to spend more time with my "new love," Norm Arno. In Norm, I continue to find great delight. He's bright and loving, a retired engineer, who shares my desire for a full life. We like traveling, boating, and entertaining in our home, but we also do what I wanted to do as a nun: extend ourselves to people in need. Those people in turn have enriched our lives.

There was eighty-five-year-old Archie, self-educated and well-read in nearly every subject. Archie lived alone, had few other friends, and looked to us only for friendship and love. At his death, we closed his apartment and disposed of his few effects. From his lifestyle we learned the value of knowledge and the relative unimportance of material things. Even now that he is gone, Archie is still part of our lives.

There was Mike, a drifter, who finally settled in Seattle at the age of forty and became a handyman in our neighborhood. His down-home insights, which I compiled into a memory book, endeared him to everyone. When Mike became sick with AIDS, Norm and I monitored him regularly. After he died, we gathered the neighbors and scattered his ashes in the waters of Puget Sound. It was a celebration of our good fortune at having had Mike in our lives. We sent the memory book to his two long-lost children so they might learn something of the father they never knew.

There's also Greta, an overburdened single mother of two small children. Greta was our friendly painter/cleaner and general handyperson, struggling to manage, when we discovered she had a four-year college degree. We coached her to find work that would capitalize on that degree, helped her tailor her resumés, and taught her interviewing techniques. She is now happily employed in her field.

These people and others like them have made us feel part of a bigger family, our own special community.

Another part of that close circle is my writing group, seven women with diverse backgrounds who came together ten years ago and still continue to meet each week. With their critical guidance, I'm working on a book about my thirteen years at St. Benedict's. Sharing my experiences with this group enables me to see my convent life in another light.

Recently I visited one of my former convent superiors in her retirement home and told her I was sorry she had always seemed displeased with me. I said I wished she had liked me. I was stunned when she said, "Oh, I loved you! But I know I failed to show it." She explained regretfully that superiors seldom had any training for their job and were simply expected to do the best they could. It was a moment of healing for both of us.

I have always been grateful for my vocation, which surely came from God. When I was a child, my parents fostered my yearning for higher things. As a nun, my Benedictine community nourished the love of learning, devotion to Scripture, and the certainty of God's personal love. Compassion for others, the need for silence and reflection, the ability to organize and lead, and a strong sense of responsibility became part of my identity.

Angie Tougas Pihlman.

With full heart, I acknowledge these ties to my past and the people who helped to make my life whole.

Angie Tougas Pihlman, *a native of rural Minnesota, lives in Seattle, Washington. She is presently writing a memoir-based novel that traces her evolution from an idealistic teenager setting out to be a perfect Benedictine nun, to the final awareness that her happiness lay elsewhere. The book's synopsis and sample chapters won second place at the Pacific Northwest Writers Conference. The Conference has also awarded her honorable mention for an essay. Retired from the University of Washington, Angie fills her days with friends, hobbies, reading, and writing.*

Chapter Nine

Learning from Benedict and Max

GAIL SCHLICHT

IT WAS A COLD FEBRUARY DAY IN 1935 when Mom and Dad, Rose and Urb Schlicht of Melrose, were expecting their fourth child. Because they already had Karen, Ann Marie, and Rosalie, they were wishing for a boy. They picked out a boy's name for this child. A healthy baby arrived. "It's another girl," said Rosalie, just over two years old, when the new baby arrived home. "She's [sic] name is Peter John." The name my parents picked for that fourth girl was "Viola Gail." Because Dad's sister, a Benedictine, Sister Viola Irene, was to be the sponsor, the new baby was given her name. For some reason, as time passed, the second name, "Gail," was the name that stuck.

In 1953, when my high school class was about to graduate, some-one had the idea that before graduation we should look up Sister Jocelyn Dubay, our fifth grade teacher. We were all very fond of her and hadn't seen her for about eight years. Several of us planned a trip to visit Sister Jocelyn at Saint Benedict's in St. Joseph, Minnesota. It was an enjoyable reunion, and as we said good-bye to her, she turned to me and said, "It wouldn't surprise me if you would become a sister." I laughed at the idea but couldn't get it out of my head. I had already enrolled in a practical nursing program in Minneapolis. I did pursue this and felt that, if I still thought about entering the convent when I finished nurse's training, I would do so. The year studying nursing went fast, and, even with the dating I had done during the year, I could not shake the idea of entering the convent. The man I was dating was not in favor of that, but he said he would not stand in the way. After graduation I polished my nurse's shoes black and entered the convent one week later. My family seemed to be okay with the idea. I was sure that after six months as a postulant and a year as a novice I'd decide, "The convent is not for me."

I liked the novitiate. Being associated with so many fun-loving people was wonderful. I even enjoyed the trips to the gladioli gardens to do the weeding or to the butcher shop to pluck the chickens. Spending time in prayer and getting to know God seemed to agree with me. As a junior sister, one of the first appointments given to me by Mother Richarda was to help

Sister Madelon in her print shop. I eventually learned to run the offset press and learned how to design greeting cards. As a third-year junior, I was sent to the Saint Joseph's Sanitarium in St. Cloud to help care for some of the retired sisters. This job was okay, but, after a year, I had had enough and knew that a steady diet of taking care of geriatric patients was not for me.

In July of that year, 1959, the year I was to take final vows, I still felt that I had no adverse feelings about staying in

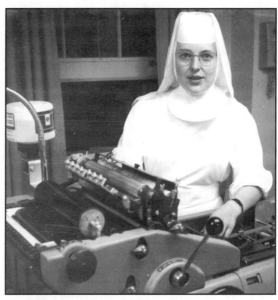

Sister Josella Schlicht.

the convent. I made final vows and was assigned to the St. Cloud Hospital. My first job was to work in the central service department. Later I was assigned to work in the operating room. My responsibilities at the hospital varied. I worked nights at the switchboard, helped with EEGs, and on weekends helped in the emergency room and Intensive Care. Then I was asked if I would be interested in setting up a print shop at the hospital since I had

had some print shop experience at Saint Benedict's. This seemed to be an adventure that I'd really enjoy. I loved every minute of it. I ran the offset press for the hospital paper, *The Beacon Light*. Eventually we acquired an engraving machine, and I made the name tags for the employees. Doing much of the printing of the hospital forms and most of the engraved signage for the hospital was really a challenge that I enjoyed very much. After three to four years of managing the print shop, I was sent to Ogden, Utah, to return to nursing. However, because I had been out of nursing for a few years, it was necessary to take my nursing boards over again. I was fortunate to be able to audit a practical nursing course at Saint Benedict's Hospital in Ogden before I took the boards.

In 1970, I began to think about leaving the community. I was now thirty-five years old and thinking that, if it was God's will, I would like to marry and have a family. This was not an easy decision to make, but after thinking and praying about it for a long time, I confided my feelings to a sister counselor. At one point she said to me, "If you really feel strongly about this, maybe you should think about leaving." I wrote to Mother Henrita Osendorf, our prioress, and told her my feelings. She wrote back telling me how sorry she was that I felt this way, but, if I was sure about it, I needed to write to the Vatican for a dispensation. A few months later I was making preparations to leave the Benedictine community, not because I had lost my faith in God, but because I felt I could be as good a person outside as I could inside the community.

In another two months, I was looking for a job in the Minneapolis area. I had spent sixteen years as a Benedictine and lacked many of the tasks I needed as a laywoman. I had to learn how to take out a loan, buy a car, find an apartment, manage my own money. I had many things to learn, on top of how to find my way around Minneapolis. My brother Chuck gave me a map of the Twin City area, and when I finished using it, it looked like a piece of lace from the wear and tear of being used and lost over and over again.

When I left the community from Ogden, Utah, I was given $200, which barely got me a few clothes and a trip back to Minnesota. I was very fortunate to have such a wonderful family. They all helped me out in many ways. Because it was two months before I began my first job, I asked Mother Henrita if I might have a little more money to help me out until I was actively employed. She gave me another $200. Since I had to have a car, I took out a loan of $2,800 from the bank and was determined to get it paid back as soon as I could. On the first anniversary of taking out the loan, I made the last payment.

When I was in high school, I had taken a class in calligraphy. As a postulant, I had taken another class at Saint Benedict's. I continued doing calligraphy through the years. When I left the community, I took another class at the Betty Crocker Learning Center in Edina. People would ask me to do one of their favorite quotations, and eventually I decided to get some better ones put on parchment paper. Later I would go to craft sales and sell them. I also had a small assortment of greeting cards that seemed to be very popular. This project was a good supplement to my income. I loved meeting all the people, other crafters as well as the people who frequented craft shows. It was my feeling that the cards as well as the verses had good Christian messages; this is sometimes difficult to find in the general card displays today.

My first job after leaving the convent was working in the operating room as a surgical scrub nurse at Fairview Southdale Hospital. I enjoyed this work and stayed there for about eight years. In 1978, four surgeons asked me to work for them in their office clinics. These were new experiences and responsibilities, and I loved the contact with the patients. It was quite a difference from seeing patients in the operating room as they were about to be anesthetized. Now I could actually talk with them about their need for surgery. In this job, I felt I was reaching many people and perhaps helping make their day a little brighter.

When I left the community in 1970, my parents were retired and in their late sixties. I would often drive to Melrose and spend the weekend with them. It was very nice to be able to take a trip with them, occasionally to Colorado or California or salmon fishing in Washington State. Now that I look back, I'm very happy that we took time for those trips.

In February of 1985, Mom, Dad, and the rest of the family had a surprise birthday party for me. It was a wonderful party, and I long enjoyed the gift they all gave me, a sheltie dog. We decided to name him Maxwell Von Schlicht. A month later, Mom died of lung cancer. I was fortunate to have been with her when she passed away. In 1988, Dad was at Saint Benedict's Center. He had been very lonesome since Mom died, and after his nap one day he died. He could not get along without Mom.

In 1989, I was off to another job, doing utilization review of medical bills. This job was more stressful, but I was able to help people find solutions for the payment of some of their extremely high medical bills.

Much of my work was communicating over the phone with patients and also with their physicians. Sometimes I felt I was not helping people directly enough. But one day a letter came from the president of the company for which I worked with this message from the husband of a patient whose bills I had reviewed: "Her knowledge, patience, compassion and faith which accompanied her comments to me were impressive to say the least. I commend her most gratefully." Though I was not working with people one-to-one, it seemed I was making some lives a little better because of what I said or did.

In 1991, I left that job because my aunt Mary Ann passed away and left her home to me, in my home town of Melrose. I had to make another big decision: should I sell my home in Plymouth and move back to my home town, or sell the home in Melrose? I was now fifty-six years old, still single, and living alone in a large city. Twice in the past few years I had been followed while walking my dog. Naturally I was frightened at times and had to be "on the alert" continually for these situations.

With my engraving background and my love for that kind of work, I decided to purchase a computerized engraving machine. I had always wanted to try to support myself with my own engraving business. I made a big decision. I quit my job, sold my town home, moved back to Melrose, and started my own business. The hardest tie to break was with the parish community of Holy Name and my involvement with the church choir. I knew this parish community was unusual, and it would be very difficult to find another like it.

I made the move to Melrose with mixed feelings. It was exciting because I'd be near members of my own family but frightening because of the fear of not being able to support myself. Certainly I had savings from working for the past twenty years, but I had to keep retirement in mind. I decided to put it into God's hands.

Many people have asked me over the years if I was ever sorry I left the community. My reply was, "No, if I had felt I made a mistake by leaving I would absolutely have had no problem asking to be readmitted." I do feel I made the right decision to leave. If there is such a thing as a "temporary vocation," perhaps that is what I had.

My life as a single person is not always the easiest. Certainly there are times when I am very lonely, but where in God's world can one be assured of never being lonely in whatever walk of life? Whether it is because of my Danish/German heritage or sixteen years as a Benedictine, I do keep myself busy, some might say "too busy." I do find much satisfaction in giving some of my elderly relatives some attention to help make their lives a little brighter.

In addition to my engraving work, I have taken on some volunteer jobs. I am currently the president of the parish council, I am the gambling manager for the parish, and I especially enjoy my work as Eucharistic minister.

In my daily travels, I find many reasons to whisper a prayer of thanksgiving, praise, and many petitions. Certainly I believe that many of these habits come from sixteen years living as a Benedictine, but I also can't fail to give credit to my parents, who were very faithful to daily prayers and always had much respect for others. Mom and Dad were great examples of honesty, generosity, and helping out the less fortunate. Mom was constantly saying, "Thank God," for something.

Today, I love to visit Saint Benedict's as often as I can for Mass and visiting the sisters. I find that the atmosphere at Saint Benedict's has changed considerably in the past twenty-six years. Immediately I notice a warm welcome that I feel is really genuine. There is an obvious atmosphere of love and respect for each other. It makes me proud to be so closely associated with Saint Benedict's and proud to say, "I am a former Benedictine." My reason for leaving the community—to marry and raise a family—was not realized. I have had a few opportunities, but, for one reason or another, something was missing for me to make that commitment. At times, I feel badly that I don't have a family of my own, but God has blessed me in many other ways. My sisters and brothers and their families include me in their lives, and I have many other relatives who are really good to me. I am blessed with good health. For what more could I ask? If God had wanted me to have a family of my own, I do believe it would have happened.

Moving to Melrose in 1991 and starting my own engraving business was a good idea. It is doing very well. I do take time to go fishing as often as my work and the weather permit. My Uncle Bob, a widower, loves to fish, so we purchased a boat together. Very often, we take his sister, Marina Plant, age ninety-two, a seasoned fisherperson, and their cousin, Father Paschal Botz, O.S.B., who is in his nineties. He is a delight to have in the boat with his wonderful sense of humor. I mow the lawn for the condo association where I live. I often see my brother and sisters and their families who live near by. I enjoy traveling whenever I can.

Until January 1996, Max, my faithful sheltie, still followed my every step. When I sat in my recliner, he was comfortably nestled at my feet. One day in January we were out walking in the sub-zero weather, and, as usual, he wanted me to throw my mitten for him to fetch as we had done so many times before. Because I was aware that he had a heart problem, I threw the mitten just a few feet. He fetched it with much enthusiasm, giving it back to me for another round. I threw it again and a third time. This time he started coughing, dropped the mitten, and climbed into a nearby snow bank and lay down. This puzzled me, and I walked up to him so see what the problem was. His eyes were open, he was breathing, but I could tell he was in very serious condition. Although I rushed him to the veterinary clinic, nothing could be done. He had died doing what he loved most, playing in the snow and fetching my mitten for me.

Gail Schlicht and Max.

Max taught me many things: what it is to be faithful and how to enjoy the simple things in life. At times I could almost hear him trying to tell me, "It's a good idea to take a little rest once in a while." I sorely miss his faithful companionship.

All in all, life has been good to me. I have had sound teachers all along the way: my parents, the Benedictine sisters, my siblings and friends, and my beloved companion, Max. May my life be a credit to all of them.

Gail Schlicht. *After thirty-seven years in the medical field, Gail has retired from nursing-related jobs and works in her home engraving business. Being her own boss allows her to vary her work hours and go fishing when she feels she needs to get away. Recently she got a new West Highland Terrier that answers to the name of "Kirby." He is a cute little thing but a real challenge, so now they are looking forward to "puppy classes."*

Chapter Ten

It's a Long Story, Charlie

EMMA ESKELSON

MINNESOTA PUBLIC RADIO IS PLAYING Tschaikowsky's "Andante Cantabile" . . . God of the dawning, God of the noontime, God of the tranquil and brooding twilight . . . as I drive down Franklin to Chicago Avenue at 5:30 A.M. on my way to work. Homeless people are out and about, the street strewn with liquor bottles, coke dealers signal for deals, cops speed by, people are lined up at Day Labor waiting for work, and another twenty or so people are standing outside until the clinic opens and they can drink their methadone before they go to work. Familiar sights now.

Unfamiliar sights in the small north central community in Todd County, which was home. I was born the oldest of five children into a Swedish Lutheran family. Having Scriptures read to us and praying together were daily practices in my family. I must have been about seven or eight years of age when I met a sister for the first time. She intrigued me, and I asked my mother about her. Mom told me that she was a woman who had dedicated her life to prayer and to doing God's work. Several years later, our family began taking instructions in preparation for being baptized into the Catholic Church. I had the opportunity to meet and to know the Sisters of Saint Benedict who taught in the elementary school and some who worked in the nursing home in my home town. Their commitment to God, to each other and to the community in which they served was a way of life that I wanted to live. I wanted to be a sister. In 1955 I decided to attend Saint Benedict's High School and was received into the novitiate after my senior year. Several years later, I began my teaching career. I loved the rhythm of monastic life—the periods of prayer and solitude coupled with life in community with my sisters. My work in the classroom was meaningful. It seemed to me that this was the way God wanted me to live my life.

I need to speak a bit about community. In one sense, it had always been idealized in my mind and in my heart. I felt I walked around on the edge looking in—wistfully perhaps—but in some deep way never really belonged. I was committed to living religious life and wanted to live a wholesome life. I buried myself in my work and became involved in working with social justice issues. This eventually took its toll. Alcohol and drugs became a refuge for me and ultimately separated me from sharing myself with the sisters where I lived. But during treatment for my chemical dependency, I became free to look at what was going on in my life.

Lesbian relationships were not talked about in community but seemed to be couched in the language of "particular friendships," which were to be avoided at all costs. But what about Clare and Francis, Ruth and Naomi, Jonathan and David, and the many deep friendships between two religious women in the community? Identifying my orientation was a painful process for me. I was told by my spiritual director, "You can't be lesbian. You like men."

In 1974, I spent some time with my brother in Colorado. One June day in early morning, I was troubled and went hiking in the mountains. I stopped by a mountain stream to rest and reached into my knapsack for the little Bible that I usually carried. Flipping it open, I read, "I look to the hills, from whence comes my help." Looking down I found a small, delicate white flower. I slipped it into my book. I was at peace.

Some sisters knew that I was a lesbian and were supportive and loving towards me, but generally I did not feel safe talking about my feelings for other women. I feared being found out.

Looking back, I believe I always had that sense about myself of being a lesbian—it was natural for me to be with women. Daring to live the truth of my life is what recovery has meant to me. Being lesbian, to me, means that my life, my energy comes from connections and bonding with other women. I also realize that my sexuality and its expression involve everything I do. My energy—spiritual, sexual, physical, erotic— is more oriented towards women—validated in community with women. Spirituality is a deeply profound human event; it is my connection with myself, with others, and with a Deity.

In leaving my Benedictine community, I had visualized and prepared a good-bye ritual in which I would come out as a lesbian woman within community. Too scary. I simply packed my bags and walked away.

I left the community in March 1988. As a lesbian woman, I could no longer philosophically or spiritually agree with the teachings of the church on women or homosexuality. Although I needed to leave my community in order to follow Jesus and to be true to myself, there is a part of me that will always remain a monastic person. The Eucharist, Scripture, and the Liturgy of the Hours continue to nourish me. Strangely enough, I believe that the Catholic Church propelled me into the lesbian community where I could walk freely, being who I truly am. I have found a spiritual home within the Community of Dignity Twin Cities, where I have been an active member for the past ten years. This community has been my spiritual home—one in which I felt whole. In perhaps a deeper way I have come to believe that God has created me as I am—with the same rights, privileges, and duties of all human beings. I did not choose my sexual orientation, nor am I disordered because of it. I believe that along with other members of Dignity Community, we are called to be a voice for justice in the Church. We are called to promote spiritual development, social and church reform, and social interaction within our communities. Being able to be *out* with my family of origin, within my spiritual community, I find the church is of great concern to me. I can no longer go back into the bottle or the closet since Jesus' teaching clearly emphasizes truth and love; one of the most basic Christian attitudes is and must be understanding the truth about myself. This is what has set me free.

I am blessed in a loving relationship with Jan, with whom I have shared a history. We have both lived the Benedictine way of life. Living my life with her feels like the most natural thing in the world. There is a rhythm in our lives. We have a strong friendship and are committed to making our life together work. We divide our home responsibilities based on our strengths. Jan is good at repairing things, doing electrical as well as plumbing work. Since my workday ends at 2:30, hers at 5:30, I do the meals and household tasks. We have the support of several gay and lesbian couples, some of whom have been in relationships for eight, ten, twelve, or twenty years. We are good at building and deepening our relationship, and that is what one does for a lifetime commitment.

Our home is in South Minneapolis. The day we moved in back in 1989, I was out by the garage when a neighborhood man came over and told me not to leave—to stay right where I was standing. Too startled to do any-

Emma Eskelson.

thing else, I stayed. A couple minutes later, he returned and handed me a very hot loaf of bread that he had just taken out of the oven, as he said, "I'm Charlie. Shellie and I live in that beautiful little white house kitty-corner behind you. Welcome to the neighborhood!" This was the beginning of a wonderful neighbor relationship with two dear people who are currently in the process of forming an intentional community in rural Wisconsin.

This neighborhood has been safe for us. I've been involved in helping organize a neighborhood block club. We watch out for each other, care for each other's sundry cats and dogs, and lend needed tools for home repair or building. One day Charlie asked me, "How do you know so much about community organizing?" I said, "It's a long story, Charlie."

We say our house has character. We spent one year refinishing the woodwork in the living and dining room. Beautiful oak wood was under coats and coats of dark varnish and various colors of paint. We've replaced most of the windows, and Jan has enclosed the front porch so it can be used for three seasons. Last summer we built a deck onto the back of the house. We share our home with three lively dogs: Jody, a year old poodle-mix, gets into more mischief in seven days than her seven-year-old sister, Buffy, ever has done. A new addition to our dog family is Kieran Michael Edward III. It takes a lot of time and love to build a home.

We have created our home in a familiar neighborhood, an eclectic one—an older woman who lives alone, retired couples, families with children, families with no children, and families like mine: two women who love each other and have chosen to grace-fully live their life together. I'll call Charlie and tell him the story.

Emma Eskelson *lives with her life partner, Jan Salzer, in South Minneapolis. She continues to work as a chemical health counselor in a county methadone program. She has been a member of Dignity, USA and Dignity Twin Cities for over twelve years, is a member of A.S.A.P. (Aids, Substance Abuse Partnership) and the Chicago-Franklin Arts Collective. She enjoys reading and taking long walks with her dogs, Buffy and Jody and Kieran Michael Edward III. Her plans for the future are to continue to work for justice within the church and political communities.*

66

Chapter Eleven

Benedictine Woman

ARLENE ZENZEN TRUSZINSKI

I GREW UP IN A FARMING COMMUNITY three miles south of Elrosa, Minnesota, the fourth child in a family of six. Mother and Dad shared the farm work, and each of the children had a particular job to do. When I started school in Elrosa in 1946 the Benedictine sisters from St. Joseph, Minnesota, had just come to staff the two-room school. My family held the sisters in high esteem. I remember Mother and Dad bringing them vegetables and chickens from our farm. As a youngster, I remember visiting my aunts, Sister Hildeburg at Saint Benedict's Convent, and Sister Rachel at St. Francis Convent in Little Falls. I enjoyed these visits and was interested in their life style.

After graduating from the eighth grade, I attended Belgrade High School for one year, and then, with some encouragement from Sister Hildeburg, I came to Saint Benedict's High School to start my sophomore year as an aspirant in the Benedictine community. I was somewhat familiar with the school and the sisters because, by now, my sister, Mary, who was three years older than I, had become a member of this Benedictine community.

Immediately after graduation from high school in 1959, I entered the novitiate along with twenty other women. The prayer and work of each day were much as I had expected and presented no problems for me. The recreation periods, during which we played volleyball and softball, were a particular joy because I was quite good at sports.

Sister Pacelli Zenzen. (Taken from *St. Cloud Hospital Beacon Light*, 1969)

During the following year, I attended the College of Saint Benedict as was the custom for many newly professed sisters. It was during that time that the sisters were asked their preference for their lifework. My choices were nursing, teaching, and missionary work, in that order. The prioress gave me the opportunity to attend St. Benedict's School of Nursing in Ogden, Utah, where I graduated in 1965. I enjoyed my student experience. In addition to the classes and the clinical experience of the regular work days, on weekends I was assigned to help in the hospital's Central Service Department or to help with patient care. The sisters had the opportunity to participate in cultural events in the area. I especially enjoyed hearing the Mormon Tabernacle Choir perform Handel's Messiah during the Christmas season in Salt Lake City. The years in Utah were generally happy years for me.

In 1965, for my first assignment after graduation, I returned to St. Cloud, Minnesota where I worked as a nurse at Saint Raphael's Home, a long-term nursing facility. The sisters and lay employees there were kind and hard-working, and we knew the residents needed us. Besides performing our nursing duties, we also took part in the activities provided for our residents and visited with their families whenever we had time. I found myself enjoying the time with family members, and I became aware of a particular man by the name of Mike, who came regularly to visit his mother. He seemed very respectful and comfortable with her and with us as he spent time playing cards, telling jokes, and just enjoying life in a very "common-sense" manner.

Gradually, as Mike and I began to develop feelings for each other, I began thinking about other lifestyles. Would I be happy in the married life? What would my family and friends say if I left the convent? I thought about it for a year and then arranged to remove myself from St. Raphael's Home, where I saw Mike almost every day as he visited his mother. I thought time and distance from Mike would allow me to give serious thought to the questions I faced.

The next few years would take me to the St. Cloud Hospital and later to Queen of Peace Hosptial in New Prague. Throughout this time I had frequent contact with Mike. The sisters were kind to me, and I made friends easily, but I knew I was preparing to leave the community. I had been very honest and open with my religious superior all these years, and, in 1970, the superior helped me obtain the papers for my dispensation from vows. I felt no real conflict or stress during the decision-making process and the actual leaving. Because of Mike, I did not foresee any real problems after leaving the convent. We knew that together we could handle any problems that would arise.

During my early readjustment to life as a lay person, I worked at Miller Hospital in St. Paul. I lived with a couple I had met while working at Saint Raphael's Home. They treated me like a daughter and helped me with any large purchases I needed. After eight months I returned to St. Cloud to work at the St. Cloud Hospital and to make serious plans with Mike for our life together. We were married on June 12, 1971, at St. Paul's Church in St. Cloud. My family participated in the ceremony along with some of my Benedictine friends.

After more than twenty-five years of marriage, I consider our life together to be ordinary but good. Because we were not able to have children, early in our marriage we adopted an eight-year-old girl. We now have two grandchildren. While there were many difficulties related to this experience, our prayer together served as the source of our strength. Prayer continues to be very important. Our morning prayer together gets us off to a good day. In addition to the prayers at meal times, the other regular prayer for me is the rosary that I pray as I drive to work each day.

Throughout the years I have continued my work in nursing. After spending ten years working in a physician's office, I returned to a Benedictine facility in St. Cloud, Saint Benedict's Center, to do geriatric nursing. This has been my work for the past twelve years. Here I talk to God often. I thank God every time I examine someone who has fallen but has no injuries, someone whose gait is unsteady but who does not fall, someone whose lab tests come back normal.

The staff at St. Benedict's Center values and practices hospitality, a charism of the Benedictines. We try to maintain a cheerful work environment, as we smile and greet co-workers and residents by name. A plaque next to the elevator has a quote from the *Rule* of Benedict: "All guests are to be welcomed as Christ." We try to make that a reality.

Arlene Zenzen Truszinski, 1991.
(From a family photo taken by Olin Mills)

In our home, Mike and I extend the same kind of hospitality. Even though our parents have died, family gatherings are important for both of us. We get together with my four brothers and their wives at our home every four to five months. Every summer we host a large gathering of Mike's family. We enjoy each other and want to keep our families united. We also enjoy the visits of some of the Benedictine sisters who have remained our friends over the years.

I feel very confident that St. Benedict has been and still is watching over me when I consider that I graduated from Saint Benedict's High School, was a member of the Order of Saint Benedict, graduated from Saint Benedict's School of Nursing, work at Saint Benedict's Center, and am an involved member of St. Benedict's Parish in Avon.

Each of these associations has been an important part of making my life meaningful and rewarding, and I am grateful for all the people who have been part of my life journey.

Arlene Zenzen Truszinski *and her husband, Mike, are active in their parish and their community. Both are greeters and Eucharistic ministers at Mass and take the Eucharist to the sick every Sunday. Mike delivers Meals on Wheels and volunteers at the VA Medical Center. Arlene has been a Birthline volunteer for many years. They celebrated their Silver Wedding Anniversary the summer of 1996.*

Chapter Twelve

If the Grass Looks Greener, It Probably Is

MARY THERESE KETTLER CURTIS

WHEN I BECAME OLD ENOUGH TO HELP round up the cattle and herd them in from the south pasture at milking time, I noticed plate-sized patches of soft, emerald green grass among the tough South Dakota prairie grass and thistle. Mom tried shyly to explain without too much explicitness that these spots existed because cows had paused and left "extra fertilizer." It became a lifelong puzzlement: how such disgusting material could make such beautiful spots, why the putrid masses were *necessary* to create them.

As I transitioned through twenty-five years of faithful effort at "*ora et labora* (prayer and work) in the service of the Lord," at Saint Benedict's and now over a dozen years in that service away from Saint Ben's, I became more and more keenly aware of that childhood lesson of the green grass.

I spent my last two years of senior high school as a boarding student at Saint Benedict's High School in St. Joseph, Minnesota. In 1957, my senior year there, many of my classmates were already "aspirants," young women trying out religious life, "aspiring" to become sisters, the first step in those days. "Joining the order" was certainly the right and best thing a young girl could do to show her love for God. Since that was my thinking at that time, I did it. Through the five years of preparation as an aspirant, postulant, novice, and junior sister, I wore the right clothes, folded my hands in the right manner, completed my chores, said my prayers, went to classes, spoke or kept silence, all at the right times and in the "rightest" way I knew. I tried hard. I must have been very annoying to people who were more relaxed and conscious of their flawed humanity than I was of mine in those early years.

I became quite adept at maintaining this striving for perfection day by day. I could, however, never imagine this as a lifetime commitment. In fact, all the years I stayed at Saint Benedict's as a student, a teacher, or as a religious educator, I remained consciously aware that I could leave, if I chose, at any time. But that would hardly be the right thing to do. I remember thinking, "I can manage until Easter," and then "until school is out" and then "until I make vows" and then until . . . whatever events would take place in the next year. During those years, I finished my B.A. degree in elementary education, taught elementary-aged children, directed small church choirs, participated in the liturgical changes taking place after Vatican II, and taught a few piano lessons. I went on to obtain my master's degree in religious education from Seattle University. I facilitated religious education programs and religious education training in parishes and in the St. Cloud diocese. I lived and worked from day to day and year to year with my sisters and friends. It took me over twenty years in the community to reach a place where I could say, "This is good. I can stay now."

And then they shouted again—the questions. Why are you here? Why are you so angry? What about a husband and family? Can you really live this lifestyle? Is this what you really choose and want?

I didn't really know what I wanted. I knew I did not experience the contentment and quiet peace within myself that I saw in my close community friends. My efforts to want to be a sister were just not strong enough any more. I finally had to let go of trying and allow the Spirit to take me where that Spirit would. So, I thought, struggled, prayed, cried, wrote, talked, listened and leapt.

It is difficult now to recall the hugeness of the growth leaps I made. I left St. Benedict's one month shy of my twenty-fifth anniversary. In fact, I signed the formal papers for leaving St. Benedict's during a class reunion with friends and sisters with whom I had spent twenty-five years praying, singing, crying, learning, teaching and celebrating. It was a traumatic event for me as we blessed and prayed for one another. I couldn't explain why, but this evolved as the course I needed to take to be faithful to my inner heart. I leapt again.

Now I had to find a job that could meet the needs of an unknown budget, locate an apartment affordable within an unknown budget, obtain a telephone number, contact the telephone hook-up service, scrounge up enough dishes to set a table for one, locate a table to put the setting on, finance a car, and manage quite a few other survival essentials. I had to learn to balance my naiveté with my enthusiasm in order to find out how the $1,000 the banker lent me actually transferred from him to my account and to the car owner. And how it would get back to him with interest through my monthly payments of $89.72. Here I was, forty-something, beginning the learning process of recent high school graduates.

I had the intense sensation of standing before a deep, dark hole into which I had to plunge. I remembered the old spiritual I used to teach, ". . . can't go around it, can't get over it, gotta go through it. . . ." I could not get to the other side of the chasm without plunging right into it. As I carried my suitcase toward the front door of my first little apartment, I remember saying, "Okay, let's go."

After milk, bread, eggs, and macaroni, I purchased a little potted pine tree to draw my eyes from the brown, utility-sized dumpster just outside my walk-out five-foot-by-ten-foot patio. This tree also served as my Christmas tree for several years. Sisters from my old home at Grace Acres, from Saint Ben's, and from my birth family, and other friends all helped warm my new home with their time, love, and care, as well as with an iron, some glasses, a can opener, towels, and other equipment for my little hermitage on Winnetka Avenue in the big city. But the grass was not too green in this season.

More than thirteen years have flown by since those desert times. I am now blessed with a generous and loving husband; eight beautiful step-children; a little black, waggy-tailed dog that follows me everywhere; a delightful, curious kitten; a nine-passenger van; and a comfortable home we built on a wooded lot in the suburbs. The grass is indeed green. Green, however, through the continuing natural process through which greenness evolves.

Community listening and living skills and training in hospitality to people and life were probably most challenged when I moved in with my new husband, four independent teen-agers, and a six-year-old. I thought I had plenty of community living experiences to take me gently into this process. However, the process became far more challenging than any of us had expected. I had to learn to accept without personal affront, the lack of enthusiasm those young Norski-mix folks had for my German-flavored treats of dumplings and tuna hot dish. As willing and eager to meld as we were, edges were firm, and we all worked hard to manage our time with, beside, and around one another. The young women were well-accustomed to arranging the furniture, placing the plants, situating the stereo in the prime focal point of the family room, and managing the household and care of their youngest brother as they saw fit. They also informed their dad about what replacements were needed in the refrigerator and when to get their hair spray. Actually, they were very good at demonstrating responsibility, creativity, and cooperation with one another. The two older boys found this quite acceptable. It gave them more time for basketball and biking. Their dad didn't even notice. With his very full-time job, this was the way things got done. For more than a year, the then small, shy six-year-old Craig remained cautious about accepting another "mom" into his life.

I, however, felt it important for us to do things together and talk over issues before decisions were made. Family meetings should be helpful in negotiating tasks and sharing conversation. I could make lists of things that needed to get done, and they could check them off as they completed each task. To my amazement, that did not prove to be the consensus. The children had managed for years without this other female in their lives, so, although they were not hostile, I simply didn't fit into their routine. I did "lose it" when I returned home from work one evening to find that the children had switched the silverware drawer to the other side of the kitchen. Actually, they had chosen a better location, but it had been accomplished not only without my input but in what seemed, in those first weeks, total oblivion to my presence and my role in the household (whatever that was).

In the ten years since the silverware incident I have celebrated with my new family/community numerous birthdays, holidays, graduations, house-warmings (i.e. apartment moves), and a wedding. Through and in spite of our experiences with car accidents, mental illness, hearing loss, heart disease, law suits, and deaths of loved ones, we gradually continue our bonding. Only three months into our marriage and move to our new home, my husband, Bud, and I were both laid off from work. Neither of us were considered "youngsters" in the work force any more.

We had hoped for a few more years and then retirement. It affected us all: children planning to attend college, we ourselves in continuing to maintain our new household, a young child with quite a few dependent years left, our own retirement funds. I took the first job offered, a clerical position in a large corporation. It provided insurance benefits and at least some income. For months Bud spent grueling hours in job search. "Terrifying" would be a mild word for this episode in our lives. The greening process has not been smooth.

What a delight now, though, to observe or participate with the children, now adults, in hiding a chocolate Easter bunny from one another or sitting around discussing trips to Europe, job changes, philosophies of religion, life goals, and what is most important in their lives. They also continue to develop excellent cooking skills appreciated by all.

Shortly after Bud, his family, and I were married, I began having dreams about Saint Ben's—the people I knew there, the chapel, the long halls, winding stairs, but I was always "visiting." I walked there, but not on the inside. I was aware, even in my dreams, that I didn't quite fit in there. I also began having dreams/ nightmares of picking things up and putting them away for the rest of my life. Little did I realize then that these recurring dreams were more than night thoughts. They became realities, daydreams, and "daymares" as my daily chores almost always include picking up and putting shoes, socks, papers, books, screw drivers, flashlights, keys, jackets in a location closer to where they originated and where they might be found next time they are needed. I notice very few items are mine. (Maybe I've discovered my role!)

As I had tried to decide on whether to "stay or leave" the community, my friend Paula had invited me to consider what I real-

Mary Therese Kettler Curtis.

75

ly wanted in the deepest, deepest part of myself. That is where the Spirit speaks most honestly. I didn't know. But I did know that where I was was not the right place for me. Yet, I didn't want to give up all I had learned and been. Paula again challenged and comforted. "Mary, you will never not be Benedictine. It's too late, too much a part of you." The question then became *how* I would live that Benedictine way in response to the very deepest desires within me. The transition, trans-mission process continues. Work and prayer remain a part of my daily life. Being a faithful steward has become a critical process for all of us. Perhaps the Benedictine "Rule" that I experience most often and strongly is that of hospitality—hospitality to adult children stopping by at unexpected hours; strangers coming to the door to sell cookies, steaks, or floor cleaners; friends needing time while they process through the dark days of their job search. I am also aware of the constant need to be hospitable to my own need for quiet, laughing and dancing through the aging process on tired, weak feet. Together and individually we continue to hope for, choose, and even welcome the greening. It is not easy, but it is certainly worth the process, especially if you take delight in soft, green grass— sometimes even sprinkled with a rainbow of flowers. I am grateful for every bit of it, the greening and the green.

Mary Therese Kettler Curtis *now lives in Plymouth, Minnesota, with her husband, Bud (Ralph), and stepson, Craig, age eighteen, Blackie, their faithful black terrier-spaniel, and Louie, Craig's curious black cat. Mary is employed as a substitute teacher and is working toward being certified as an ESL (English as a Second Language) teacher. She enjoys reading, caning chairs, and refinishing old furniture. Bud delights in antique cars and feeding birds in their back yard. Together they like gardening, "antiquing," and looking for a winter place farther south.*

Chapter Thirteen

Don't Sweat the Small Stuff

SIGRID HUTCHESON

WHEN I WAS TWENTY, AND CELEBRATING my first Christmas in the convent, my mother was inspired by a current TV show to give me a photo album captioned, "This is Your Life." The pictures in the small booklet chronicled my life from my birth in 1937, through the annual photos of the first day of school, high school band, graduation, heading off to college, the first summer job away from home, and ended with the last days at home before leaving for the convent. Looking back at these pictures I remember all the best of those twenty years of my life. Growing up on a traditional family farm near Goodhue, Minnesota, we had plenty of farm work and housework and no such thing as a vacation. However, there was lots of fun fit in around the edges and many imaginative adventures with my brother David. Since I was an end-of-the-Depression baby, we had very little cash, but I was never conscious of feeling deprived. Whenever I wanted something that we couldn't afford, my Mother's response was to say, "Well, let's talk about it again next week." Of course by the time the week had passed, my fancy had shifted to something else; I had usually forgotten what was so important about last week's request.

I entered the second era of my life when, in 1957, after attending the College of Saint Benedict for two years, I decided to become a member of the convent community. I had been watching the sisters while I was a college student and was intrigued by their happiness as well as their sense of purpose and commitment. When I decided to ask to join the com-

77

munity, I believed that everyone else in the community had probably known since they were children that they were called to religious life. I was not at all sure they would even accept someone who was so slow in deciding to join, but I still wanted to try. When I was accepted I remember thinking that I would undoubtedly be the least qualified person in the group, but that maybe if I tried very hard I would be allowed to stay. When we went through the decision point on December 8, I fully expected to be told I was being sent home, and I wasn't sure if I would feel sad that I had to leave or happy that I could stop trying so hard.

In the following year when we became novices, I began to really enjoy myself. The manual labor and outdoor work, including the potato gathering, turkey butchering, and bean picking were what I had grown up doing. Saint Benedict's admonition to "Live by the work of your own hands" was a natural as far as I was concerned. In this year, I learned for the first time the delight of having close women friends, and I remember with great joy the closeness of those relationships. I loved the classes and the whole rhythm of the life and felt I had made a good decision.

In the years after the novitiate, I was blessed with a wealth of opportunities for professional growth both through work experience and education. I finished college, taught sixth grade, and completed a master's degree in chemistry at the University of Minnesota. A few years later, when it came time for final vows, I again, on one level, hoped to be turned down, so that I could leave gracefully. Somewhat to my surprise, I was accepted into full membership in the community.

I continued to have varied educational opportunities, challenging work assignments and interesting living situations. I taught at the College of Saint Benedict and held various administrative positions. I received a master's degree in educational media from the University of Colorado and a doctorate in higher education administration from Syracuse University. We lived through all the post-Vatican II turmoil with endless debate about the details of what we should wear, how we should live, what work we should do, and how we should pray. It was not a dull time. Like everyone, I went through times of discouragement and doubt, and I saw many of my friends choose to leave the community. Caring, concerned friends in the community were always there, however, to support me through the hard times.

Yet, as I approached the end of the second twenty years of my life, the sense that I was not really successfully meeting the challenge of being part of this community began to be overwhelming. I looked around me and saw some of my sisters who were not happy and were becoming more locked into their unhappiness as they grew older. That was the future I feared for myself. I simply was no longer up to the struggle of trying to be good enough to be a worthy member of this community I had grown to love, respect and admire so much. I did not want to stay in the community if I couldn't be as good a member as the community deserved. So, in 1978, at the end of my fortieth year, I chose to leave.

In the nearly twenty years since leaving the community, I have married, lived in Ann Arbor, Michigan; Albany, New York; and now Washington, D.C. I have had interesting jobs, including being assistant to the dean at the University of Michigan; director of Management Information Services for the New York State Office of Mental Health; and senior policy associate in a Washington consulting firm.

Creating a life with another person has brought into focus the influences of my first twenty growing-up years and the almost twenty years in the community. I marvel at my good fortune in finding a husband who grew up in a totally different setting as the oldest son in a family of six children of a Baptist minister. Yet, even with our differences, we share many values and ideals. Since I am now almost to the end of the third twenty-year period of my life, I am beginning to look ahead to retirement and the changes that will bring. As my husband and I talk about how we want to retire, we find that we are articulating our priorities in life more clearly than ever before. I am conscious again of the many ways my time in the community is continuing to influence my decisions:

First, hospitality—One of the first things we realized when we married was that we both wanted a warm and welcoming home, where people would walk in the door and instantly feel at ease. I think that is what Saint Benedict meant by receiving all guests as Christ. We have created five such homes, and regularly welcome friends for an evening, a day, a weekend, and long periods of time. We have often housed people who were moving to town and needed a place to stay while they were looking for a house; our home became their home. Now, in Washington, D.C., we are the home base for friends and acquaintances coming to see the sights. We find great pleasure in having mastered the art of making guests feel welcome.

Second, community life—During my life in the community, I learned how to live happily and comfortably with a tremendous variety of people. The analogy of a bunch of stones in a bag rubbing the rough edges off each other as we go to God was always real for me. In practice that meant for me "not to sweat the small stuff." I have often remarked that after living for years with several hundred women, living with just one man is very simple. But one of the things that makes it simple is that there are many little things that are simply not worth making issues, and a few important things that are worth real time and energy. My husband and I have the deepest respect for one another. We both dread the experience of being with couples who demean one another in public or engage in hostile or cutting remarks about each other.

Third, moderation—My husband tends to be a plunger, while I am more of a plodder. When we do serious hiking, he dashes ahead and then stands there panting, waiting for me to trudge up the hill to catch up. He would take off all the wallpaper in the house at once, and then spend months restoring civilized living conditions. I would do it very methodically, one room at a time. We continue to strive for balance in our lives, but I have quoted Saint Benedict to him so often over the years that moderation is becoming more of a way of life for us.

Fourth, stewardship—We share an attitude toward things. We seldom purchase major things like furniture, but rather prefer handmade things, family heirlooms, or treasures brought home from foreign journeys. Nearly everything in our home was chosen for a reason, and most things have an interesting history. We value these things that have meaning, and sometimes treasure them so much that we give them as gifts to special friends.

Fifth, work—I have had interesting jobs in universities, state governments, and not-for-profit firms. With each move I have started the job search knowing I don't care what I do as long as it is interesting, worthwhile and teaches me something new. I am still finding opportunities that meet my criteria. Of all the roles I have played, the one which has brought me the most pleasure and satisfaction is serving as a supervisor. I love working with a diverse staff to discover their talents, involve them in work assignments that challenge them, and then work hard to get the obstacles out of their way so they can succeed. When I left New York State government, at the going-away party where people say nice things, I was most pleased at how many people indicated that they always felt I really listened to them and that they knew they were valued and respected. I think Saint Benedict would have been proud.

Sixth, church—One of the hardest adjustments for me when I left the community was, and still continues to be, finding my place in the Church. One Sunday about six months after I had left the community, I was sitting in church and realized that I was no longer in the in-group. As a member of a religious community I had a designated place in the Church, and, while I certainly was not part of the hierarchy, I did have a place with a label. What a jolt to realize that I no longer had such a place but rather was just part of the undifferentiated mass of the laity! Over the years I have struggled to find a place in the Church where I am needed and at home. I have not yet been successful. I believe, but I don't feel I belong.

Seventh, women—The most profound and persistent influence that Saint Benedict's had on my life was the result of living and working in a community run by women and for women during the most formative years of my adult life. I have watched women in the workplace struggle and agonize over issues of perceived inequity and disrespect. Often they were unable to distinguish trivial issues from serious ones, and were not able to separate their own ego needs from matters involving real wrongs. The security of having lived and worked in a women-friendly environment has given me the wisdom to choose my battles carefully, use a response proportional to the issue, and ignore the incidental things. I also learned that no matter how close my husband and I are, I need close women friends in order to be happy and live fully. I can see now that this is a lesson many women never have the opportunity to learn. Currently I work in a small, woman-owned consulting company in which all eight professionals are women. At the end of my first week, the president was startled, but I think pleased, when I told her I loved my job and hadn't had this much fun since I was in the convent.

Sigrid Hutcheson.

Four years ago, when Saint Benedict's had a reunion for all those who had left over the years, I attended with mixed feelings. I had left the community in the era when leaving was done openly with plenty of advance notice. In spite of that, much had gone unsaid before my departure, and I had not seen most of the members of the community for almost fifteen years. During one of the discussion sessions, I had the most important insight of the weekend for me. I left the community because I was overwhelmed with a sense of no longer being able to live up to what was necessary to be a full and productive member. At the weekend gathering, I looked around and was struck at the number of talented and gifted women who had left over the years. I realized that the community needs to find a way to harness some of that talent back into doing good for the community. I have, for example, developed management information systems, done research on health policy issues, conducted evaluations, delivered management training, and written successful grant proposals. There must be some ways the community can use some of that experience even though I am no longer an official member. Many of us who have left the community still feel connected to it more strongly than those who are still in the community may realize. We would find great joy in being able to serve the community both using what we learned as members and what we have learned since leaving. For me the real shock was realizing that, in contrast to how I felt when I left, now the community needed me. I have gone from feeling unable to live up to the community's ideals to having something to offer that the community needs and values. What happened in the intervening fifteen years to turn my thinking around? It is simple. I am married to a man who every day of my life tells me I am wonderful, who believes in me and supports me, and occasionally suggests to me how I might have done something better.

As we look ahead to our next twenty years we are hoping for a welcoming home, preferably in a temperate climate, furnished with things we treasure, with things to do that have value, in a setting where friendships can grow, and ideally in a Christian community where the values that have shaped our lives will continue to flourish.

Sigrid Hutcheson *and her husband, David Chapman, spent a number of years in Albany, New York, and have just completed a three year adventure in Washington, DC. Life in Washington was exciting and provided many new challenges, but last year they returned to Minnesota searching for a less intense life style. David is a professor at the University of Minnesota and Sigrid works part-time for a Washington company consulting with state governments on information systems and on mental health and substance abuse programs. She also has time for volunteer work and involvement in Democratic party activities, as well as for enjoying her extended family and friends from earlier eras of her life.*

Chapter Fourteen

Walking among the Saints

JEANNIE M. WEBER

MY LIFE TODAY

I LOVE MY LIFE! My work fits perfectly at this stage with the person I've become. Currently I work as a recreational/activities therapist at St. Therese Home, a 302-bed, long-term care facility in New Hope, Minnesota. We have a Benedictine inspired mission statement and some Benedictine sisters on staff. I am still very much Benedictine at heart. My life outside work is replete with rich social contacts and ministries through my very vibrant parish community of Christ the King in Southwest Minneapolis. During these past sixty years, I have been in touch with a very mothering God who has been guiding me and healing me. I am "at home" on my way to my permanent home.

I am blessed with four growing, searching young adult children, each on an individual quest for a life path: Tony, a linguist, historian, geographer with special interest in world soccer; Vince, well on his way to becoming a physicist in Colorado; Maria, pursuing interests in art, design, and humanities; and Theresa, with strong humanitarian interests, studying psychology and Spanish at the University of Notre Dame.

My job challenges me to enhance the quality of life of the very old and sick. It provides me a daily opportunity to live the call of the gospel, practically without effort. My people are given to me. I only need to open my eyes, peer into their souls, and let love, friendship, and reciprocal relationships flow between us. Each resident comes as a living treasury of history, experiences, gifts, and diminishments. I try to see, bond with, befriend, and love each person by searching for and being receptive to his or her individual realities. It is easy to love and appreciate each of them. My work is often physically demanding. I have to approach it with a great deal of enthusiasm to entice the residents to remain engaged with life and become an active part of the community in their living area. On the other hand, I often experience the life-giving power of work. At the end of the day, while my body may be tired, I usually drive home with a happy heart and a head that is already thinking of how I will serve the residents and their families better tomorrow. I hear the echo of Jesus' call and promise: "I have come that you may have life, and have it to the full."

Coming to St. Benedict's

My family lived in California when I was born, the second oldest among seven brothers, and the only daughter until my youngest sibling, Margie, came along just when I was preparing to leave home. In California I enjoyed an outdoor, active life in the sunshine of the Pacific and the beauty of the mountains. These early experiences taught me a love of nature and physical fitness. My mother introduced me to her God, the all-loving, ever-forgiving, ever-enabling, joy-filled Spirit who yearns for our fullest development, healing, and happiness. She taught me, through witnessing, that the God-Spirit pervades our being, walking with us at every moment, coaxing us to choose well, to feel gratitude for our giftedness, to gather wisdom, and enjoy wit, to share with our fellow travelers a shoulder to lean on. Mom lived this belief. She prayed often, probably always. Mom taught me to immerse myself in the sacrament of the present moment. She said (and I often say to my residents), "Yard by yard, life is hard; inch by inch, life's a cinch."

Daddy was strong-willed (more like stubborn) and liked to control, but he also loved life and was quick to laugh. It was Daddy's influence, in large measure, that led me to Saint Benedict's. When his dad died, he retrieved from among my grandpa's treasures a homely plaque made in the 1930s by one of the sisters from St Benedict's. It read "I'm the Daddy of a Nun." My grandpa's daughter was Sister Aloysius Weber, OSB, former supervisor of schools (of whom the children used to chant "Holy cats and holy fishes, here comes Sister Aloysius!"). When I asked my Dad why he was keeping this plaque, he replied simply, "Well, some day I may be able to hang it on my wall." Sister Aloysius' presence in our home for many weeks during my Grandpa's dying of cancer, acquainted me, an impressionable grade-school child, with this gentle, joyful Benedictine aunt. It nurtured the desire in my heart to always be close to God and to live a life of service to God's family. That daily prayer for vocations after Mass and my Catholic girls' high school retreat on vocations further fed my sense of obligation to at least offer myself to God as a religious and to allow Him to lead me.

Other strong influences in my early formation were my awareness of being fully accepted and loved by my family, teachers, and schoolmates. Both my parents and my many younger male siblings looked to me for leadership, guidance, insights, and understanding. I was tutor, barber, baby-sitter, seamstress, and all around big sister to the boys. My parents treated me like a third parent.

Daddy thought I could do anything. He encouraged me to lead the way, think my own thoughts and create my own life. He used to say, "Be an iconoclast." The experience of this kind of unconditional love was very empowering.

Living in Community

We moved to Washington, D.C., when I was beginning high school. I loved the new life, made lots of new friends, and had a very satisfying school and social life. In the summers, we lived on the Chesapeake Bay where I was a camp counselor, swimming instructor, and the community barber. Outside of work I enjoyed sailing, water skiing, canoeing, and having fun in a wonderful carefree environment. In the summer of 1959, after my second year in the Bachelor of Nursing program at Catholic University, I toured Europe with a group of college students and young teachers. My travels took me to Holland, Germany, France, Switzerland, and Italy, including a visit to Monte Casino, St. Benedict's own monastery. Then I returned home, broke my informal engagement, gave away my custom-made water skis and all my belongings, and came to St. Joseph, Minnesota. I had never lived far from an ocean or in a rural setting. The change for me was earth-shaking. I couldn't decipher which differences were rural, Midwestern, German or convent, but I knew for sure that this was a different world.

Community life, however, was a natural for me. I loved the social aspects of togetherness in community. I learned to appreciate the structured time for prayer and reflection, study, work, recreation, sleep, and meals. I fell in love with Minnesota's changing seasons, the fields of waving grain, the whisper of leaves, the wonder of hoarfrost, and the awesome Aurora Borealis of the North Country. This was a radical change for me, but I plunged into my new life with one-hundred-percent effort and enthusiasm. But, most of all, I was profoundly influenced by the gentle, holy, good women—the saints among whom I was privileged to walk.

As the second oldest of nine children, I was a second mother, so care-giving was my first calling. After coming to St. Benedict's, I studied nursing at St. Mary's Hospital and the College of St. Scholastica in Duluth, and cared for the elderly sisters in the infirmary on "Broadway" at St. Benedict's. However, as my nursing career began to lead into more administration, it became clear that hands-on care with close interpersonal interaction rather than administration was my talent and my delight. I studied sociology at the University of Michigan in Ann Arbor, and then completed my MA in sociology at the University of Notre Dame. I became a high school teacher of social sciences and loved working with the students while attempting to engage them in the process of learning.

Community in the abstract means little. However, it was the women with whom I lived in community that enfleshed for me what Benedictine community and the living communion of saints meant. They had a profound influence on me as I struggled to become one of them.

Our director during our initial year in the community was fragile and gentle, but used prayer and reliance on God as her supports. She called forth cooperation from us and pleaded for us to find the best deep within ourselves. I found friends who were instant sister-soul mates in the community. We bonded immediately, understood each other intuitively, and spent countless hours sorting out life and pondering its meaning together.

St. Benedict's Gifts to Me

During my twelve years as a member of the community at St. Benedict's, I had many experiences and opportunities that I treasure. They continue to shape my life.

• I had previously only experienced life with brothers, so the experience of sister love was an unexpected joy.

• I learned an understanding and love of the psalms and scriptures, along with the beauty of Gregorian chant and prayerful meditation and contemplation. The verse from Psalm 46:11 continues to call me. "Be still and know that I am God."

• I had an opportunity to explore careers from nursing to education and to complete a Masters degree in Sociology at Notre Dame.

• I discovered the life-giving power of work, and learned that work, well done, can be a prayer. I worked closely with sisters who truly lived by the work of their own hands in the kitchen, farms, and gardens.

Sister Martin Weber, 1964.

• I found my voice. I learned to love to read and sing aloud, and have used this gift in the classroom, church, and now in the care center.

• I learned to take a more organic view of my faith. In my early religious education, truth had been presented as static and fixed by what we heard from the pulpit and read in the Catechism.

• My theology teachers opened my mind and heart to scripture, liturgy and most of all to the theology of the mystical body. They taught me to appreciate oneness while treasuring diversity. The *Rule* of St. Benedict encourages followers to receive all guests as Christ.

• Philosophy classes challenged and stretched my intellect and fed a life-long yearning to probe the mysteries of life, beauty, goodness, and truth.

• When I was teaching I had principals and colleagues, who mentored me, encouraged me and enabled me to succeed as a fledgling teacher.

• In my years of formation in community, I was blessed with directors who modeled discipline and determination, showed single-mindedness of purpose, and were filled with wisdom, common sense, joy, and confidence.

Here and Now

I left St. Benedict's in 1969, twenty-nine years ago, because I wanted a family while still living out the call of the gospel. I have fulfilled my life-long dream of being a mother, that profound joy of creating and nurturing life in the body, mind and spirit of children. When I became a mother, I realized that parenting combined what I had learned about care giving and teaching, both at home and at St. Benedict's. One of the most meaningful supports I received when my children were young was teaching in the Tiny Seed Experience in my parish. This program opened scripture to very young children, those tiny seeds of the parish community, trying to nurture the tiny seeds of faith in them.

Now I am pulling back from the intense, daily attention of hands-on motherhood as my children each launch their own adult lives.

I find myself exercising my Benedictine convictions in my parish involvement in welcoming new members into the community, engaging in service and social justice outreach, participating in Interfaith Hospitality Network for temporarily homeless individuals and families, and serving as Eucharistic minister and lector. One faith backbone for me is the Remember Group, a house-church which reflects on scripture and theology and shares life lessons in mutual support of one another. My new sisterhood is a group called Woman-Spirit, which I joined and which has become a continued life-blood of spirituality for me.

My current greatest fulfillment is in my work, where I continue to walk among saints. My job at St. Therese Home is an extension of the mission and purpose of the Benedictines. I try to live out a vision of creating a community of residents, family members, and staff who can rely on one another and enjoy love and laughter together as we try to improve the quality of life for our seniors. I try to serve every resident so that each can say and feel with confidence that:

- I am safe (I will be protected and not neglected).
- I am needed.
- I belong.
- I am cared for (My needs will be noticed and tended to).
- I am loved as a member of God's family.

The very old residents with whom I work often seem to be more complete and fully human than their younger counterparts, even though they are somewhat diminished in certain physical and mental capacities. They are more mature in spirit, more fully "in bloom" as human beings.

When I look at my current job and consider why I love my work so much, I realize that much of the joy comes from it being a culmination of many of the forces that have shaped me throughout my life. I am living a summing up of the best of what I have learned and experienced. My dad was always ready to laugh, and I have been blessed with the same disposition. "Serve the Lord with gladness," has always seemed right to me. In the difficult times in my life, I have tried to remember that humor and laughter are very healing.

My care center community empowers me by returning love, affirmation, and appreciation. What could be more enabling? I feel my calling is to try to energize others and to empower and enable people around me. My role in life seems to be to envision the hope and then attempt to create the reality.

My life today is a blend of my growing-up years with my parents and siblings, life in community at St. Benedict's, and my life since leaving St. Benedict's. All these influences merge into who I am today. Some values and principles permeate my whole life, initiated by my parents, nurtured throughout my life, and now realized most fully in my work and parish life. These values can be distilled into the following six values, which are all explicitly called for in the *Rule* of St. Benedict.

Jeannie Weber, 1998. (Photo by Proex)

• Need for and love of community. That they all may be one.

• Joy of hospitality/welcoming. Receive all guests as Christ.

• Reverence for all people and all creation. Treat all things as sacred vessels of the altar.

• Focus on prayer. Pray always; seek God in all things, persons, experiences, and nature.

• Value of work and creativity. They are most truly monks when they live by the work of their own hands.

• Sacrament of the present movement. Walk always in the presence of God.

At the end of my life I expect to be asked just one question: How have I loved? I know I have learned to love from the saints with whom I have walked. My goal now is to continue to live out the love I have observed and experienced throughout my life.

Jeannie Weber *lives in Bloomington, Minnesota, where she maintains a home for her four college and graduate school children to visit. She is a recreational therapist at St. Therese Nursing Home in New Hope, Minnesota. Her life is rounded out by her active participation in the community life and ministries of Christ the King Parish in southwest Minneapolis.*

Chapter Fifteen

Benedictine Always

ANNA KLEIN

*"This is what I call 'slumming it'," said Tom as he and several other
of my graduate school friends helped carry my few boxes and many plants
up two flights of stairs and into the attic apartment I had rented.*

*The cloudy, cold day in Iowa City in 1972 was typical of February.
The attic apartment contained a bed and dresser, table and chairs, and two
old stuffed chairs. It smelled musty, dusty, and closed up, like an attic. The
kitchen area had no sink. A washbasin stood in full view across the living
area. There was no bathroom in the apartment. The bathroom downstairs
was to be shared with tenants on second floor. The last tenants had taken
all except one light bulb which was shining above the top flight of stairs
inside the apartment.*

AFTER SOUL-SEARCHING SEVERAL YEARS while teaching mathematics and
statistics at the College of Saint Benedict and Saint John's University, I
had decided to live a year of exclaustration while taking classes toward
my doctorate at the University of Iowa.

There were many things for me to learn. I had entered the Convent of Saint Benedict in 1957, immediately after high school. Fifteen
years later, apartment hunting, grocery shopping, and living on a budget
were all new to me. My teaching assistantship in the Statistics Department paid $400 a month. After tuition and apartment rent, I had $200 left
for utilities, food, books, and all other living expenses. Since there were

no assistantships available for summer, it was also necessary for me to save money to pay summer school and living expenses for three summer months. This was real poverty.

Frugal living was part of a life of poverty in the convent, and those lessons were well-learned. Nothing was wasted. Walking was a way of life. I had no car. Since Iowa City was a university town, many students walked. The single-minded purpose for my life at this time was getting an education. This focus was shared with many fellow graduate students.

That first night I walked to the grocery store to buy light bulbs and a few groceries.

A year and a half later, in 1974, I left the Convent of St. Benedict for good. The seventeen years I spent at Saint Benedict's have had a wonderful influence on my life. I am certain that my life now would not be as good had I not devoted those years to God and community. I have never regretted the years I spent as a nun at Saint Benedict's.

* * * * *

"Wichita State University is looking for a director of their Testing and Evaluation Center. Did you see the ad in The Chronicle of Higher Education?*" Doug Whitney, my dissertation advisor, asked.*

"If it were anywhere except in Kansas," I told him, "I'd apply."

I did apply for the job and was chosen for it. Wichita State University would become my home.

The following situations illustrate the influence that the Convent of Saint Benedict has had and continues to have in my life outside the convent.

While I was in Saint Benedict's, I was involved in the liturgy, beginning with Gregorian Chant in the 1950s through English choir music and planning the Liturgy of the Hours in the 1970s. Throughout graduate school in Iowa City, the liturgy continued to be important in my life. I had been active in planning and singing at the Catholic Student Center. The choir director at Blessed Sacrament Church in Wichita had a reputation for using good music and achieving quality rendition. Naturally, I moved into Blessed Sacrament parish so I could sing in the choir. It met all my expectations. During the twelve years in that parish I also participated in the liturgy as a lector and was instrumental in obtaining five octaves of hand bells to supplement the adult choir, liturgy books for the congregation, and an electronic keyboard for the youth choir. Later I moved to Andover and became involved in the liturgy at St. Vincent de Paul Church there.

Recently I spent the winter in a small community in Mexico. In addition to attending Mass at the Catholic Church, I attended a non-denominational community church service. I have been part of a group introducing praise songs into the liturgy. We had one "Praise Sunday" a month. In February, I received approval from the board of directors to have a Vespers service on Sunday evenings. We are planning to start this program next winter.

* * * * *

"If I buy a coke, does it come out of my ten dollars?" my little sister asked during a gas stop on our trip to Minnesota.

"Yes, but there's water, orange juice, and tomato juice in the cooler. That's all free."

Being the oldest of ten children, I had lots of experience as a big sister. Since we grew up on farms in Minnesota, we learned the value of family and how to have fun together.

At this time, I was living in Wichita, was forty years old, and had no prospect of getting married. It was clear that I would never have children of my own. So when I heard the local Wichita television advertisement for the Big Brothers/Big Sisters program, I volunteered. I had my own ideas on what was important in a child's life. Rather than spend our time together going to movies or being entertained, we usually entertained ourselves by cooking, baking, sewing, gardening and doing other things that would be educational for my little sister. We planned things that she did not have a chance to do with her mother.

The two of us took various car trips. During these trips I would pack a cooler full of fruit, sandwich makings, juice and raw vegetables. An eleven-year-old girl would rather drink coke and eat junk food. To solve this dilemma, I gave her an allowance of ten dollars a day while we were on a trip. That money was hers to spend as she wished. She learned fast and had enough money left over during each trip to buy gifts for her family.

* * * * *

"I need to talk to you. Do you have time now?" my acting dean at WSU was on the phone. "I'll be right over to your office," he said.

"The Testing and Evaluation Center will be closed on July 1 this summer," I learned during that February meeting. "The Mathematics Department needs a statistics teacher next year," he said.

Playing politics has never been my strong point. I have learned that everything is politics. Not only government, but corporations, educational institutions, the legal system. When I decided to leave Wichita State University, I knew I had to start my own business. I established a Financial Services business, which I operated for eight years, until 1991. I thoroughly enjoyed this business because I felt I was helping people. The closing of the Testing Center was the push I needed.

Before finishing my college degree in mathematics while at Saint Benedict's, I taught first grade at St. Anthony's School in St. Cloud. Later, while completing my coursework in mathematics, I did student teaching under Sisters Evin Rademacher and Joyce Williams at Cathedral High School. I taught mathematics and physics at Cathedral for the next five years.

Sister Evin was our superior most of my years at Cathedral. She introduced us to Yoga exercises, which I still do today, and small study groups which I didn't appreciate at the time, but which benefited me in many ways. Work, rather than my religious community, tended to dominate my life. Preparing physics classes and laboratory experiments, advising the Camera Club, and attending St. Cloud State University (then St. Cloud State College) after school to prepare for graduate school in mathematics took so much of my time that I didn't take time for community. I worked alone. Through Sister Evin's small study groups I learned valuable aspects of working with others.

My teaching background was helpful in Financial Services since I taught classes, seminars, and individuals how to make the most of their money. It was very rewarding. I put in many hours learning a new field.

One tenet of my business philosophy was, "Don't be afraid to do something for free." I believed that if I gave something, I would get back one hundredfold. The classes and seminars I taught were free. Anyone who took one of my classes could have a free consultation and financial plan. My newsletter, which I compiled six times a year on the average, was free by request. My clients ranged from one who was on ADC (Aid to Dependent Children) and welfare to another who received a one million dollar legal settlement.

"Knowledge is power" was my approach. I felt that it was important for my clients to understand their personal finances. One of my supervisors said that my sales approach was, "Educate them to death and hope that they buy." Probably quite true. Now I was teaching all day, usually on a one-to-one basis. However, not all of my efforts at helping were successful.

When I married my husband, Les, I found myself in the midst of family problems that I have not been able to solve to my satisfaction. This has caused much pain and disbelief. Family values I learned in early childhood and confirmed in the Convent of Saint Benedict make it difficult for me to comprehend some of the things that happened.

Another disappointment occurred when Les and I took into our home a man who had been in and out of prison all of his life. He was Les's neighbor while his children were growing up. Les thought that perhaps this person really never had a chance. We wanted to give him a chance.

We let him move into our extra bedroom. We bought him clothes, helped him get his driver's license back and get a job. I loaned him an old car I had with the understanding that he would make monthly payments to me after he had a job. He lived with us rent free until he could get on his feet. Our joint goal was that he would find an apartment in three or four months.

Anna Klein. (Photo by Prism Photography)

Everything seemed to be going well. When he got a job working as an electrician, we visited him on the job. I was volunteering my time teaching classes in the Singles' Program at the local Methodist Church. He signed up for classes to get acquainted with other people his age.

When we took an extended leave from our house in January, we asked him to stay and care for our pets. However, he got back on drugs. He allegedly robbed businesses to support his habit. Furthermore, and we have not been able to understand this, he pawned tools, jewelry, electronic equipment from our house to get money. He had a gun in his possession when he was arrested. He is now back in prison, and we have not seen him since his conviction.

Other ministries in which I am currently engaged include flying mercy missions as a private airplane pilot, taking food and clothing to the Mexican Indians during times of need, working to correct problems in the current application of the judicial system.

Benedictine life has had a lasting effect on me. There are several aspects of monastic life that I took for granted while at Saint Benedict's but which have become important outside the convent. "Moderation in all things" is important for everyone, not just monastics. I find myself saying this on many occasions.

Daily meditation is something I took for granted, and in which I even engaged reluctantly at times. Now I find it an important part of daily routine. I seldom miss my morning meditation; the day just doesn't go as well when I oversleep or miss it for some other reason.

I am forever grateful for my sisters at Saint Benedict's and the influence they have had on my life.

Anna Klein *now lives in Kansas and frequently flies to Mexico where she does volunteer work with churches and non-profit medical facilities. She continues to fly medical missions, enjoys reading and writing, learning Spanish and helping others in many ways.*

Chapter Sixteen

A Thing of the Heart

CLARE CALHOUN RITCHIE

I AM THE THIRTEENTH AND LAST CHILD of my parents and was born during the Great Depression. These were hard times, but I do not recall feeling poor, perhaps because most everyone those days was poor. I lived in a big house, had food to eat, plenty of family to look after me, and good playmates. What more could I ask? Many of my memories through grade school center around church—pretending we were priests and nuns, attending church, singing in the choir, attending church ice cream socials, participating in May processions, and enjoying some of my Benedictine teachers. I attended a Catholic grade school but there was no Catholic high school in our town. When I began high school my horizons were expanded by making friends and having teachers who were not Catholics.

After high school I became a secretary-bookkeeper and moved to Colorado. Here I worked hard and had lots of fun. The beauty of the Rocky Mountains was a constant inspiration to me. I began to feel, however, that there was something more to life than making a living and having a good time. I got involved in volunteer work, but it was not enough. I prayed to know what to do with my life. During this time, my sister, a Benedictine nun, asked me to take a visiting nun on a sight-seeing trip of Denver. I was at a loss to know what to do with a nun, but I did show her the sights and took her to see a family that she knew. Seeing this beautiful family made me think I wanted to be married and have a family of my own. However, after she visited me, the nun sent me a brochure about the Benedictines at St. Joseph, Minnesota. Its emphasis on community life appealed to me. After reading it, I knew I wanted to join that community of sisters. I felt positive that my prayers were answered and that I was called to be a Benedictine. In 1958 I joined them.

It is difficult to sum up what thirteen years in the Benedictine community did for me. The novitiate was a time of getting to know myself and God better. I wished everyone could spend a year like that in preparation for marriage or whatever way of life he/she might choose. In the earlier years three things in particular stood out for me. Though I knew love was what mattered most in life, it was particularly enlightening and meaningful to me in Scripture class when our novice mistress, Sister Henrita Osendorf, wove the thread of love through the Scriptures. The second thing is how life in the community opened me up and widened my vision to extend to my universe. The wonderful diversity and quality of women in the community expanded my sensitivity in so many ways—to beauty, music, poetry, cultures, ideas, above all to the beauty and wonder of a human person. Another theme that became a part of me while in religious formation was that of poverty of spirit. I saw Mary, the mother of God, as a symbol of poverty of spirit—of being open to the immensity of God and of wanting nothing but to magnify God.

Sister Mary Clare Calhoun, 1964.

If my formation and community life meant so much to me, why then did I write when leaving that I no longer found meaning in it and felt it would be dishonest to stay? While in the community, I finished college and taught high school. After three years of teaching, I convinced the prioress that I was not an effective teacher. In 1967, after receiving a grant for a masters in social work, I went to graduate school. While there, I had permission to wear lay clothes because of my therapy work. I was reminded of how "normal" and responsible it was to live in an apartment, make money choices, and be among lay people. During this time, a love relationship developed between me and a priest.

After graduate school, I began work in family therapy. I was happy with my work, but, in the community, I began to feel discontent. It was after Vatican II, and there was much opposition to change within the community. I began to feel this opposition personally. I had been allowed to be without the veil at school, but now, though I was working as a full-time therapist, I was required to wear it again. After repeated requests to go without it, I received permission but only after writing the prioress that if the veil was the essence of the religious life I wanted no part of it. After repeated requests, I also was allowed to live with a small group of sisters with a designated budget and our own daily schedule of prayer, work, and recreation. At the time I left the community, I was living with three other sisters in an apartment near my work. When I served on the committee for setting up a retirement plan for the community, I met with resistance to my ideas to set up a retirement center for the elderly sisters. I also recommended that more sisters earn full salaries to plan for the future.

An article I wrote on the essence of religious life shows that I was deeply questioning that life. In it I stated that the essence of religious life was a thing of the heart and that all the vows we took could be boiled down to the one Benedictine vow of Conversion—change of heart—choosing to put on nothing but the heart of Christ. I saw each of the vows as a matter of the heart firmly committed to Jesus leading one to a life of simplicity and sharing (poverty), a life of openness to love, intimacy, and acceptance of others (chastity), a life of trust in the Spirit to know God's will (obedience), a life of constancy and loyalty to the community (stability). Furthermore, that focus on the vow of conversion would prevent our getting lost in the externals of religious life, which are perceived to be safer and more secure but may keep one from living at the heart of the Christian way of a pilgrim—moving, changing and not having time to build walls of protection.

It is easy to see from what I have written that I was struggling with the emphasis that I felt was being put on the externals of religious life. Wearing a habit, living in an assigned group setting, observing religious customs are among the externals of religious life but not the essence of it. Questioning these externals created bitterness and ill feeling among community members who did not understand the need for change or were threatened by it. I experienced this personally because I had been the first in our community to wear lay clothes; I was among the first to live in a small group; I had a love relationship with a priest and was not secretive about it. I became tired of working for change and came to experience the community as an institution that made too many decisions based on preserving the institution rather than on considering the individual person. I felt disillusioned with community. It was a combination of these things and the storm that my love relationship with the priest stirred up in me that made me become interested in marriage though I always knew it would not be with him. Here I felt some dishonesty—though I was still physically a virgin. My heart was not living the "spirit" of my vows. I talked to the prioress, went on retreat, prayed to know God's will for me and, in 1971, made my decision to leave.

In many ways my transition was easy because I continued in my same job. I was already in lay clothes and was managing a budget, much like before entering the community. After a year, I realized that my only relationships were with my religious friends so I thought it best to move. I applied for a number of jobs around the country where I could enjoy either mountains or an ocean. I accepted a job within an hour's drive from my priest friend. I met my husband indirectly through a valued friend in the community. I believe that was providential. I am married to a very good man whose wife died and who had three children. My priest friend officiated at our and our daughter's wedding, baptized our two grandchildren, and is a very dear friend of all our family.

When I left the community, in my heart I did not give up the vow of conversion, and I still feel a loyalty and love for the community. I was not foolish enough to believe I would not have struggles after I left. They were just different ones. After moving away, I experienced the loneliest time of my life and found little satisfaction in the Church. I have had varying degrees of involvement with it. I once served on the Parish Council and was head of the liturgy committee. The five-day parish renewal I planned had as the theme "Turn Around"—conversion. I also gave a talk on Mary after Mass in preparation for a May procession. I do not often return to the Scripture for my spiritual life but take with me that woven thread of love that runs through it to guide my daily life.

As a therapist, I was governed by one main principle: to refuse to label the person I was helping. Labeling causes one to look at people within a narrow framework, which makes it more difficult for them to move into the expansiveness of conversion. Post Vatican II days in the community taught me to look to the heart of people and accept them as they are.

After marriage I had a part-time private practice but was mainly a housewife and mother. The vow I made at my wedding was to grow in love of my husband. I also needed to grow in my love of my new family. The mother role was not easy. It took me a long time to let go of the desire to feel loved by them and to trust that what really mattered was that I loved them and that they would feel it.

Clare Calhoun Ritchie, 1997.
(From a family photo)

I now work as a hospice volunteer visiting terminally ill people. There have been many deaths in my own family. While in the community, I was with some of my Benedictine sisters as they prepared for death and died peacefully. I do not fear my own death so long as there is no unforgiveness in my heart.

I have experienced periods of deep sadness over issues of social justice particularly relating to the poor, over the unforgiveness in so many hearts on individual, family, national and international levels and over a lack of respect for God's creation—God's environment and God's people. I attribute this to the sensitivity that developed in me during my years in the Benedictine community. I try to counter this sadness by simplifying my life, sharing some of our wealth, being an avid recycler, feeding the birds, squirrels, and woodchucks, composting, and above all, looking to the heart of everyone.

My life is comfortable with a loving husband, family, travel, friends, and many welcome guests. It is one of moderation and an integrated balance of short prayer, meditation, exercise, work, and play. For what more could I ask? I feel there is something more. I know what it is. I hunger for immensity! I do not love enough. My heart and the hearts of countless others are not yet at one with our God. Until all our hearts "turn around and around," until we are all one with each other and with our God there will always be something more.

Clare Calhoun Ritchie *and her husband, Wally, are retired and live in a condominium in Salem, Massachusetts. Clare continues to be active as a hospice volunteer and has become interested in Reiki. She remains connected to the Benedictine community through her friends there. Whenever she is in Minnesota she and her husband spend time at St. Benedict's.*

Chapter Seventeen

Seeker

MARCELLA TAYLOR

MY TIME AT SAINT BENEDICT'S WAS ONE OF CHANGE. It was the sixties, when Americans were re-examining values that seemed to lead to racial injustice, social division, and a devastating war in Asia. The "open window" of Pope John Paul XXIII was causing joy or consternation, depending upon one's point of view. Some at Saint Benedict's advocated dispensing with the rule of silence, donning modern dress, meeting less frequently in chapel for the hours of the Divine Office, reciting the psalms in a conversational tone and interacting more with the world around us. I was ambivalent.

I had been drawn to Saint Ben's because of what the monastic life promised. I agreed with the need to jettison the superfluous and the obstructive, but what others often considered out of date I saw as shaping the soul of our existence: a ritual language, solemnity in the recitation of the Divine Office, a day punctuated by rhythms of prayer, work, and study, designated times of silence and solitude. Yet, ironically enough, at the end of the decade, I would leave the revolution inside the convent to join the political, social and cultural one taking place outside. I would desert Bernard and Marmion for Marx and Marcuse, explore Duchamp and Cage, watch Fellini and Godard, join circles that passed around a "joint" of marijuana, participate in women's poetry readings, create "happenings," cheer at rallies that condemned Vietnam, racism, sexism, and the destruction of the environment, attend pentecostal gath-

101

erings where some spoke in tongues and I danced with a companion to boisterous renditions of "Lord of the Dance."

Was this inconsistent? Perhaps not. It followed the impulses of my childhood and the motifs of my heritage—African, Creek and Celtic. As a child during World War II, I watched a truck pass our gate filled with Highlanders playing "Road to the Isles" on the bagpipes, and my soul thrilled to the music. We sang British folksongs, but I was most fond of such airs as "Loch Lomond" and "I Love a Lassie." I read many British novels as a child, but my favorites were Sir Walter Scott's. Unconsciously, I was the child of my father, a Scots-Bahamian. Too, I began to recover that wider heritage represented by my mother's people as I discovered more exotic places between the covers of books—Africa, New Zealand, Argentina, China, the Eskimo lands, and that of the other Native American tribes. I traveled through time, pausing long in the medieval world, riding with Arthur's knights, worshiping in some huge cathedral.

Side by side with all this was the religion that framed our family life in Nassau. I can still hear the lusty singing of the Mass of the Angels at Sacred Heart Church, smell the incense and feel the cooling breezes awakened by the motion of ceiling fans. Our lives were never divorced from the Church and the Benedictine monks who served as our pastors. Father Denis and Father Arnold, who served at Clarence Town, Long Island, in the Bahamas where I was born; Father Ambrose, our first pastor in Nassau; and Father Charles and Father Alban, who followed him.

It was Father Alban Fruth who became pastor during my adolescent years, but now we were worshiping at St. Bede's, a new parish closer to home. The women of our family became the mainstays of the parish, decorating the altar with flowers every Saturday. At the early morning weekday Mass, I often read the epistle from my place in the body of the Church and, when there was no altar boy, I recited the Mass responses. No wonder I later mourned the loss of the Latin.

Through the loan of books, Father Alban acquainted me with the mystics and the Fathers of the Church: Saint Augustine, Thomas a Kempis, Julian of Norwich, John of the Cross, Thomas Merton, the *Rule* of Benedict. The two threads of my life merged in the world of the medieval church, the worlds of artifacts and of religion. Father and I spoke of vocation, and he sent me to see Sister Alfreda from Saint Benedict's, who was visiting the Sisters of Blessed Martin de Porres in Nassau. I was not interested in joining this group, who lacked a long tradition, or the Sisters of Charity who always seemed so uncomfortable with our "Bahamian" ways. But I pored over the Saint Benedict's brochures Sister Alfreda left with me. A year or so later, however, I left to attend college in Pennsylvania.

When I had returned to Nassau and lived a social life ranging from a cocktail party on a United States naval vessel or a dinner at Government House to weiner roasts on a moonlit beach or skating parties by Lake Cunningham, I still found time to visit Saint Augustine's Monastery and enjoy conversation with the monks. After I became an Oblate of Saint Benedict attached to Saint John's Abbey, Collegeville, Minnesota, it was inevitable that I again felt the tug of the monastic life. I pulled out those old Saint Benedict's brochures and told Father Frederic that I wished to enter Saint Benedict's. Always the clown, he countered, "Are you sure you don't want to join the monastery?" He was right, of course. I wanted to join the monastery. I made plans to join the Sisters of St. Benedict in St. Joseph, Minnesota. My entrance date was almost a year later, and, in the meantime, my heart kept doing flipflops. I loved Nassau. I could never understand those who waited only for the chance to leave it. I walked my old haunts with tears close to the surface. I was not afraid of assuming a new life, but I consciously mourned the passing of the old.

I always felt an urge to embalm the past so that the present would be less two-dimensional. In Iowa City, years later, my psyche played with futuristic images, but when I found myself yearning for revolution, I saw a reinstatement of the good lost over the centuries as well as the institution of what had never been tried. What I didn't want was the "everyday" that seemed to be taking over the convent milieu in the 1960s, the sense that we must become like everyone else. I saw myself as other, my destiny to be daring and nonconforming even among the nonconformists. Iowa City with its noises of social revolution, avant garde art, experimentations in lifestyle, and close-knit communities (we spent a lot of time "being there" for each other) called to me.

Yet it was Saint Ben's in its communal life that was my true novitiate for life in the world. It nurtured me, developing my psyche on many levels, and gave me a larger vision of the world than I possessed when I entered. While I came to the convent equipped with lessons from my father who brought party politics to the Bahamas, the debates at Saint Ben's in both informal discussions and formal deliberations were my apprenticeship in the doing of politics. Later, too, when I had moved out of the sisterhood, I was more prepared than most for that other one, the Women's Movement. After all, weren't convents even then a bit like the legendary isle of the Amazons?

In the convent I could expand the reading and study begun beneath the roof of that house on Shirley Street where I grew up. I supplemented the novels and the poetry, the geography and the history with philosophy, theology, psychology, astronomy, art history, and theory. I read works translated from German, French, Italian, Greek, Spanish. I encountered other writers—Tagore and Eliot, Jung and Eliade, Maritain and Mauriac—and had my first wonderful teaching experience, Greek and Roman Classics in Translation at the College of St. Benedict.

At the age of seven I had written my first verse, lines that made up in passion what they lacked in craft. My poems were confessional and my mentors suspicious of my style, too unlike Auden and Eliot, then in vogue. Later, when I read the poets of my years in the convent—Plath, Sexton, Lowell, and Berryman—I recognized my own poetic impulses. I celebrated my final profession of monastic vows perusing the sensitive response from the poetry editor of *Commonweal*, who had accepted my first poem to be published nationally.

At Saint Ben's, my reading and writing fed and were fed by the life of the spirit. I had learned to meditate before arriving and knew what it was to feel God's presence. But now the space and the mentoring deepened this sense of the eternal that could pervade our lives, to allow it through ritual and reflection to frame each day. I still evoke that presence listening to the St. Paul Chamber Orchestra or walking a strange city street or glimpsing a cardinal on a branch of my backyard sycamore.

The gift of appreciating nature so deeply came to me from Saint Ben's. In my childhood, true nature was abundant—fruit trees crowding our backyard, roses, oleanders, frangipani, chrysanthemums, bougainvillea circling the house, and palm trees covering the island. Birds flitted in tree branches, and fish swam in the bluest water in the world. I took it all for granted. Bathing in the ocean, staring out at the harbor, I watched fishermen and their boats. At Saint Ben's I saw how our natural world gave birth to the other, the making of artifacts, the revelation of spirit. Now the campus is marked by the architectural beauty of new buildings. Then, the land and what it birthed dominated, buildings nestling unobtrusively into the setting. I loved walking the grounds, pausing to sit and read and, most of all, to stand at the entrance of the woods, ready to plunge into the world of the Scandanavian fairytale. I think my life would have been blessed if it had been allowed to continue to be shaped by the lawns, walks, shrines, the little pond with its lily pads and tiny fish. But I left.

From the distance of years, it is hard to name the definite event that catalyzed my departure. I took a leave of absence, almost certain I would return, but, at the end of the year, I realized I was at home, content with the life I had assumed. There were contributory reasons. I was concerned about family needs, about what I had begun to see was my desertion. Too, I had been told that on completion of my studies I would need to farm myself out to some other Catholic college; there was no teaching position open at Saint Ben's.

I did feel claustrophobic in institutional life. My soul was uneasy in the outer confinement of motion, the inability as I saw it to follow detours that called to me. After my final profession of vows, there seemed to be no more milestones ahead. I wanted uncertainty, the unknown tracking me. Away from the convent, the claustrophobia disappeared. In the counter-culture world, I still nursed my emotional turmoil, but it was transformed through tears, existential irony, dance, poetry, and noons gazing at the Iowa River, Kiekegaard on my lap. Anguish was a cheap trade-off for the gift of life.

One of my superiors suggested that I couldn't make the decision to leave the community because I saw the Church as a parent and felt safe only in her bosom. But reading over my journals from that time, I know it was just the opposite. I was never afraid to move out into the world. My journals testify to my desire to be allowed to grow. I applied for a summer program in Vermont and prayed hard for acceptance, a time apart from the cocoon.

My worst moment at Saint Ben's was Christmas Eve of our novitiate year, when we were given brightly wrapped gifts opened amid hysterical laughter and then told we would have to rewrap them for next year's class. Not that I wanted to keep mine. It was the silliest of all, a bedraggled figure of a monkey because I was from the Bahamas.

Twenty-four when I entered, I sought older companionship, but, when I was finally allowed it at Cathedral High School, chasms opened up beneath me. It was not simply that I felt intellectually constrained. I was totally adrift as we moved through the antithesis of a monastic day with its heavy load of teaching with all that teaching entails. Where was the romance I had sought? Where was the healthy rhythm of life laid out by the *Rule*, days with equal parts of prayer, work, study, and rest? My incursions into monastic lives from Julian to Merton had not prepared me for this. I felt exiled from the motherhouse, and when I knew there was little chance of my returning, I felt I had been given my license to leave.

Disturbing memories scarcely surface. I remember the friends I made, and I stay in touch. I take what I learned and I move on. I study, teach, write. I adopt a nephew, sustain good relationships and lasting friendships, and sometimes let go. I make many opportunities to travel and settle comfortably for a time into life in Dijon or Florence or Chicago. Sometimes I wonder what it is all about, these dislocated moments, disjointed events. Where are the solid achievements, the discernible patterns? Friends admire my eventful life, and when a good friend from Dijon articulated his envy, I countered, "It doesn't mean I have been happy."

Marcella Taylor.

He thought for a moment and then recited an anecdote: A reporter once asked Sophia Loren if she was happy, and she answered, "I would not think that happiness is what life is about. Rather, it is about experience."

Was that what my Scorpio nature always craved? I still ask: has this experience all been random, or am I still on the seeker's path? I find myself ferreting out what seems right, both for self and world. I move into active politics, but I am disheartened by a lack of passion in the process. My mind returns to Saint Ben's, and my heart sets to wondering. I still sense that the monastic life is the true life of the seeker.

Well, then, I remain a monk. I grasp moments of beauty as I move on my journey, the hills of Umbria that made Francis sing so sweetly, the Taos sunsets that roof the earth like a dome of fire, the dark green vegetation and white and yellow blooms that arc to meet the multiple greens and blues of the Clarence Town harbor. I treasure whiffs of zen-like peace as I wash dishes, await a friend in a Grand Avenue coffeeshop, listen to jazz in the Dakota, curl up on a couch in my faded Victorian livingroom to read and listen to Aztec music, walk the aisle of Lund's searching for the right sauce for a dinner party, or attend Midnight Mass at the St. Paul Cathedral. Then I think it doesn't have to get any better than this. I contemplate another move. I give up my tenured professorship—no, not to retire, but to move out into a life more diversified, more adventurous, more filled with intimations of what lies beyond our pilgrimages. I hesitate. Perhaps it is too late. I am too old. But that forest of the unknown waits. I am attracted. No, not any longer by the lure of filling the voids of my life. I no longer live in the hope that it will all come together. Once, when I bemoaned that my life seemed filled with obstructions so that I have not fulfilled my true identity, a friend responded, "But how do you know that what has happened to you is not exactly what was meant to happen?"

I say, "Amen." Perhaps Saint Ben's taught me that. That what is given is destined. I will again take those first steps along new roads. I should be afraid. Yet I don't think I am. I have done this before.

Marcella Taylor *lives in St. Paul but dreams of traveling more in the next five years in France, Scotland, and New Mexico. She recently received a Jerome Travel and Study Grant to spend six months in the Bahamas. In St. Paul, she continues to write and to work on projects with arts organizations and the Minnesota Jung Association.*

Chapter Eighteen

A Bird of the Pines
A Parable

PATRICIA VINCENT PICKETT

ONCE UPON A TIME, IN A TOWERING GROVE OF PINES, many beautiful and wise birds lived in harmony. In this realm lived a young bird who was exceedingly curious. Her name was Seeker. Seeker's history was uncertain as she had been found wandering at the base of a noble spruce one spring morning after a pounding storm. Cherish, a red bird, found her. Cherish brought nuts and berries to the frightened fledgling, coaxing her to shelter under her great red wings when the north wind blew.

In time, Seeker was able to fly. She felt comfortable among the others and found her own rhythm of work and song. There were many times Seeker questioned the ways of the older birds, but they were patient and schooled her in the ways of communal living.

As time went on, Seeker grew restless and begged to fly beyond the boundaries of the pine trees. No one could change her mind. On the day she was to leave, Cherish, a yellow bird named Wonder and Grace, a lovely blue bird held her close. Each placed a small gift in Seeker's knapsack. "Do not open these gifts today. You will know when the time is right to use them."

Seeker felt as though her heart would break . . . she hugged all three and, without turning back, flew to the top of the giant spruce and followed the glow of the setting sun.

Her flight separated her from all that was familiar and propelled her into the unknown. Soon the skyline changed, and she could no longer see or smell the pines. She trembled, resting on the limb of an oak. As the darkness closed in around her and rain began to pelt the tree, her thoughts raced back to the pines. She missed the safety and warmth of those great red wings, remembering how Cherish would cradle her when she was afraid. As she pictured Wonder, imagining her unique song, the rushing wind became a melody. And then, Seeker sensed the peace of Grace. As she snuggled in the hollow of an oak, Seeker thought about the pines. Perhaps she never should have left. Perhaps she had made a mistake. Sleep soon dissolved her troubled thoughts.

It was spring. Seeker felt an urge unknown till this time. She began to gather sticks and twigs and bright pieces of string. She wove a brilliant nest in the oak. She had never made a nest before, but it came easily as she remembered watching Wonder weave elegant decorations from pine needles, bits of bark, and wild flowers. Her nest was strategically located in the crook of a strong limb. It protected her from most storms. Seeker had not noticed another bird watching her industry. In time they became friends. It felt good to feel the warmth of another bird. It seemed so long since Seeker had left the pine grove filled with birds.

Seeker did not understand her bulging body. One sunny day that question was answered. Seven speckled eggs lay in the cup of the nest she had so carefully woven. Something told her that she should stay put, but that was all she knew.

Seeker remembered the knapsack with the gifts. "A good time to explore the contents," she thought. Opening the gifts, she discovered red fluffy down. Cherish must have plucked the softest feathers from her own body as a gift to Seeker. Seeker carefully lined her nest with the down. Next she opened the gift from Wonder. It was a tightly closed yellow bud. Before Seeker twined it among the twigs of the nest, she tried to open it, but the petals would not budge. Seeker had so little patience! Wonder was wise. She had given a gift with potential. Small as it was, the bud's lovely fragrance filled Seeker's world. Finally, she opened the gift from Grace. It was a pine cone. Seeker smiled. Of course Grace would send food for the journey! Just as she was about to settle in for a nap, the nest began to move. Just a tremble at first, then such shaking that Seeker perched herself on the edge and turned to look inside. To her surprise there were seven perfectly formed miniatures of herself. And they were hungry! A real dilemma! How could Seeker leave the little birds to look for food? Seeker rearranged the soft down. They seemed to be comforted. She remembered the pine cone and fed the little birds a few of the tiniest seeds. Satisfied for the moment, Seeker knew her babies would soon be hungry again. She flew off for berries and delicious bugs.

As the days turned to weeks, Seeker discovered many uses for the gifts from Cherish, Wonder, and Grace. The gift from Wonder continually changed. Little by little the bud was opening. One day she could use it to catch rain water. Another day it became frilly tail feathers, which she used to entertain her young, pretending she was a great parrot with yellow ruffles. The bud was extraordinary in its color. Seeker noticed how its shade and hue changed with the temper of her nest. It reminded her to teach her young ones to recognize the colors of compassion and tolerance, peace and justice, inclusivity and self-respect. She taught them to look beyond what they could see, using all of their senses in discovery. Seeker taught her brood the fragrance of loyal friendship and the aroma of generosity. She taught them to balance their days with song and work.

With the gifts from Cherish, Seeker learned to insulate her young from the violence of the outside world until they were old enough to protect themselves. She nurtured them as she had been nurtured. Seeker was comforted by the memory of Cherish as she patted the soft down. She noticed how tufts of it had grown to the babies' speckled feathers.

Grace's gift helped them all grow strong. They were nourished with the food from the pines. But baby birds would be baby birds! The seeds made wonderful flying objects to sail through the air. They spun when tossed. If thrown just the right way, gentle winds would carry them out of reach. This is the way the babies learned to fly. Seeker would throw a seed and the young ones would scramble after it, often tumbling out of the nest. It surprised each when the wind caught their wings and brought them back to the nest. At first they trembled, then they chirped, tumbling out of the nest, never going very far. Then, one or the other would venture out of eyesight. Seeker would warble them home before dark, and one by one they landed unceremoniously and snuggled together for sleep. One summer evening none of her babies came back. She knew each had begun his or her own adventure. Seeker snuggled in what was left of the down and buried herself in the fragrance of sweet baby smells, or was it the ever growing flower from Wonder? There was an ache in her heart, though she knew that this is how it should be. Had she not learned in the pines that loving is being able to set loved ones free?

Seeker woke from a fitful sleep. Fierce wind was bending the oak. Lightning crashed. She reached over to tuck her young ones under her wings, only to realize they were gone. Were her babies safe? Had she taught them well enough? Would they forgive her mistakes, real or imagined?

When the storm passed, Seeker felt a yearning to move again. It was hard to leave without her young. She packed the red down, yellow flower, and pine cone. She looked lovingly at her nest. She turned toward the horizon where dark clouds were forming. She flew for hours, through lifetimes of storms and unbearable heat. She could smell the fragrance before she could see it. A mulberry tree! Gratefully, she drifted to the uppermost branches. Here was supper *and* bed!

In the morning, Seeker was startled by a loud and angry racket. Perched high in the tree, she could see the whole forest floor. It seemed alive with color. Birds of every shape and size, long feathers and short, striped, polka-dot and madras were swarming in panic. Seeker moved closer. From what she could gather, there had been a fire and birds lost their nests and familiar food sources. She thought of her young ones and hoped they were safe. Her thoughts were interrupted by a strange silence that fell on the bevy of birds. Seeker caught the sight of *purple*. Hundreds of purple birds on the forest floor! These purple birds chirped with an air of authority. No one seemed to be in charge, and yet they all seemed to be in charge. Seeker could not understand the fuss. It seemed so simple. From her vantage point she could see red, blue, green and orange berries only inches above their heads. It was time to intervene! She fluttered to the ground and began, "Excuse me, sir, but I can help you feed this kin of ours . . . why . . . ."

A rather officious purple bird stepped forward. "You cannot possibly help us feed this crowd. Don't you know that for all eternity it has been decreed that only purple birds may decide how to feed others?"

"How silly," thought Seeker. She was undaunted. "But, sir, it is so simple . . . all you have to do is fly up a few inches! Apparently you have eaten all you can reach . . ." Seeker realized that the purple birds could no longer fly. They had become so fat, they could only waddle. Seeker thought to herself, "All of us who have fed young ones can certainly help feed this crowd. There must be others here like me."

"Be gone, foolish bird. You are not of the purple. Your color is only a misbegotten accident. Only the purple have served food to others." Seeker laughed out loud. Silence fell over the covey. The purple birds turned to see the audacious warbler.

"Are you going to deprive these birds of food because you cannot see beyond your beaks? I am not of the purple, nor do I want to be, but I have fed my brood and shared with anyone who visited my tree without knowing your rules. These birds will die without food. You will die because you seem to have forgotten *why* you eat and *why* you feed!"

With that Seeker flew to the top of the mulberry tree. She flew for days without looking back. Then, without warning, the oak which had sheltered her as she raised her young, appeared in the distance. It looked different. She giggled to herself. Of course, the seeds which her young had used to toss when learning to fly had fallen on the ground. Now they were growing trees! Seeker landed on the top of the oak. She was startled by the "swish" of other birds landing with her. Many of the birds from the forest had followed her. She was happy to see them and have them share her space. There were even a couple of purple birds in the group who had been carried by the others.

As she reflected on her journey, she realized she had an opportunity to pass on new life to others. She also knew that some of these nameless others would be profoundly touched by Cherish, Wonder, Grace, and the many birds of the great pine trees through their gifts to her. Seeker had thought her work was finished when she launched the last baby from the nest. Caressing the red down, yellow flower, and pine cone, she understood she was forever, a bird of the pines. . . .

It is ironic that I am more Benedictine today than I ever was while in the community. It was not the *Rule*, but the relationships with women who lived the *Rule* that made the difference. The Benedictine way of life is alive in me because there were women who risked a relationship with me even though I was young, immature and unpredictable—women who prayed with me and for me, laughed with me and were unashamed of tears, women who argued, nurtured, taught, corrected, counseled, hugged me, women who were sometimes proud of me and other times disappointed in me, women who loved me without expecting anything in return. Many women touched my life while I lived in community. There are those whom I will never be able to thank. There are those I do not know except through their example and the story of their lives passed on to me.

There are three women, in particular, who have continued a relationship with me through the years. Each in her own way has been mother, sister, friend, confidant, spiritual guide, and peer. Each gave and gives generously of herself. Their gifts have become part of who I am today. I am able to love my own children because I learned what it means to be part of a family through the love of "Cherish." She loved me when I felt no one else in the world cared whether I lived or died. I am able to stretch my own creative gifts toward their fullest

Patricial Vincent Pickett, 1996. (From a family photo)

potential because of "Wonder." She never expected less of me than to be in awe of all creation, even when I was hurting. It is her intuitive beauty that helped me discover my own. My faith as a Christian is ever enriched because of "Grace." I have learned to stretch the boundaries of the institutional church in order to answer God's call, constantly attentive to the words of Benedict, "Listen carefully, my child, to my instructions, and attend to them with the ear of your heart." *Rule* of Benedict, Prologue.

Pat Vincent Pickett *is the mother of seven grown children and the grandmother of four. She is a writer and liturgical artist. She has worked in pastoral ministry in ecumenical settings that include American Baptist, United Methodist, Presbyterian, and Catholic. While ministering in the inner city, Pat founded, with several others, a program of reconciliation for buyer and seller prostitutes. Currently she is chaplain at Clover Bottom, a state institution for the mentally and physically challenged. Pat holds a B.A. degree in sculpture and design from Metropolitan State in Denver, a masters in Religion Education from the University of San Diego and an M.Div. and D. Min. in Hebrew from Colgate Rochester Divinity School. She has written, costumed and blocked a liturgical ballet to her dissertation,* The Anger of a Loving God.

Chapter Nineteen

Thy Will Be Done

Carol Deml Sisterman

As a child I dreamed of marrying. My sister Cathy and I spent time planning our weddings while we cleaned the chicken house or as we built our "grass clipping" homes after mowing the lawn. Cathy talked about being a sister some day. Not I! I was going to be married.

In 1958, I spent fall and winter quarters at the University of Minnesota. Before spring quarter began, Dad wrote inviting me to attend a vocation day with Cathy; he suggested that I might "become a nun"; I laughed. But because I respected Dad as a wise man, I heeded his words.

At the vocation day, I met many sisters from a variety of communities. Sister Patrick Joseph Flynn was the one who attracted my attention. Her warmth personified the spirit of the Benedictine community. She wrote to me that summer, sending information about the community and encouraging me to join. I prayed, "Thy will be done."

I registered for fall classes at the university. Somehow that decision did not feel right. In tears, I went to tell Dad I wanted to join Saint Benedict's Convent in St. Joseph, Minnesota. I was afraid he might be angry with me because I had already made plans to go to the university, and changing them would be a bother. But his response surprised me, "I always wanted one of my daughters to be a nun." When I arrived at Saint Ben's with my family, it was the evening of the college pageant. I was impressed by the sisters' pride in sharing their Benedictine history in this annual event enacted before hundreds of people.

After joining, I wondered whether I had made the right decision. Was the Spirit really calling me to this way of life? What is your will, God? The first year I talked with my postulant director, Sister Catherine, about leaving the convent; again the next year I talked with my novice director, Sister Mary Cecelia. Each of these women urged me to continue pursuing this Benedictine way of life. I obeyed because they were wise women whom I trusted. On profession day we lay in a prone position on the floor as we made our oblation to God. I promised Jesus that I would follow Him wherever He led but in my mind was a reservation about following Him in this way.

During my nineteen years in the convent, I discovered Benedictine values. Communal prayer and work offered balance and structure. As a novice, I thought that if I ever left the convent, I would always be grateful for this structure.

We were given instruction on how to pray the Scriptures during our private prayer time. This was a challenge because it required setting aside time simply to be quiet in the presence of the Lord. It meant listening and becoming familiar with this God whom I could not see. Over the years, this Scripture-based private prayer has given me a glimpse of the depth of God's love and goodness.

Eucharist and communal prayer cemented our relationship with God. Shared meals, an extension of the Eucharist where we became imbued with God's love, were opportunities for God's presence to be made present in our relationships with one another. Around the dining table, I listened to and shared with many, many women over the years. I made many friends; I learned from the wisdom of the elderly; I was inspired by the enthusiasm of youth. I cultivated a respect for differences of views, sometimes not an easy thing to do.

Through many opportunities provided by the community, I learned to know myself. I taught elementary school children for ten years. Teaching was always a struggle for me because I did not have the gift of teaching, but, because I was asked to do this by the prioress, a wise woman, I had obeyed. During those years, I joined the charismatic prayer group at the college. While taking the "Life in the Spirit" seminars, I was touched by the personal interest of my instructors. In particular, I was moved to tears when my college instructor, Sister Emmanuel, whose intelligence was awesome, prayed over me.

When I expressed a desire to work with adults, Sister Patrick Joseph, then personnel director, sent me to a pastoral ministry program in Denver, the completion of which led me to an interview for a position in pastoral ministry in North St. Paul. I met Father Bill Sisterman when he, along with two other priests and three laymen, interviewed me for the position in April 1972. Being interviewed by six men was a heady experience, and, when I was invited to join the team there, I was elated.

Sister Patrick Joseph, again listening to the Spirit, alerted me to a clinical pastoral education quarter at Abbott-Northwestern Hospital, which I took before I began my new assignment. By counseling people on the medical-surgical floors and in the psychiatric ward, I learned how I related to adults. I learned that I could hear "no" and say "no" without a sense of rejection. Having gained trust in listening to my inner self and confidence in my self-worth, I joyfully plunged into my work in North St. Paul.

Although I loved my work, an inner sense of unrest settled upon me. Where do I belong? What is your will for me, God? In the early months at North St. Paul, I shared this question with our prioress. After two years, she requested my return to Saint Benedict's to become vocation director. Obediently, I accepted this new challenge, but I had not anticipated living in the college dormitory with young women. My need for community with the sisters was not satisfied, and I was disappointed, lonely, and depressed. After two years of service, the prioress told me I would not be vocation director the following year. This was very painful because I loved working with the women who were seeking God and because she gave me no reason for this change. I didn't ask why; but I obediently accepted others' decisions for my life without question. Thy will be done?

In the next two years I served as pastoral minister in two different parishes while I still searched for peace. During my thirty-day retreat and during another retreat later, I called Father Bill, who suggested talking over a meal. Even these times were unsettling, because I seemed to be testing my limits relationally with this man. Please, God, Thy will be done.

Finally, I called on the help of Sister Henrita for counseling. Over the course of a year she listened to the Spirit at work in me. We looked at my early years of wanting to be married.

Could this really be my call? Is God's will for me to leave this community of sisters? Could I leave the convent and all its comforts, safety, and familiarity? Could I risk the possible scorn of the people I loved? Sister Henrita did not give me answers; she asked me questions, which helped me stand on my own inner resources. My answer to all these questions was "yes." It was scary. It took courage. But praying the

Scriptures time and again, I had heard, "Do not be afraid"; "I will never leave thee or forsake thee"; "Take courage."

The evening I told Sister Evin, then prioress, of my decision, she said simply, "Now you know your direction." That night I dreamed I walked over a bridge into a field, a broad expanse like that in the movie, "The Sound of Music," where I heard the singing of alleluias. Here was peace. This was right. Later, as I reflected, I realized that dream occurred on the Feast of Pentecost

The sisters helped me in my transition with a car and money. I went to Sister Delarene to give her my ring and my prayer book—a ceremony of departure. She graciously accepted them from me, telling me she would miss me. I knew I would miss St. Benedict's. The things I missed most were community prayer and conversations around the dining table, the communal relationships with God and the sisters.

I needn't have worried about telling Mother and Dad my decision; they were very supportive and even invited me to live with them, but I wanted to make it on my own, no matter how hard it might be.

After I left Saint Ben's, I stopped to visit Father Bill. As usual, we went somewhere to eat. Over breakfast, he told me that he would not leave the priesthood but would continue with his vision of building the church, placing one brick upon another. What an awful blow! Painful and lonely as I knew I would be, I knew I could make it without him. I told him that I would not call him anymore. I spent a year grieving.

But I did not die of grief; I continued living. I had grown to love Benedictine history and decided to visit the roots of Saint Benedict's community in Eichstatt, Bavaria. As I prayed in the town church attached to the cloistered community, I was unknowingly locked in the church. I panicked. Frantically, I checked all of the doors. None would open. Standing in the center of the sanctuary, I shouted, "God, I don't want to be here." As I checked another door, I saw two bars, one up high and one down low. They slid aside. I was free to go. Visiting Eichstatt was an experience I'll never forget. It reaffirmed my decision to follow Jesus outside religious community life.

I dated, but with no prospect of marriage. "Thy will be done," I wept in prayer, asking God for someone I could treasure and cherish, someone who would treasure and cherish me, who would share my values. "Remember, where your treasure is; there your heart is also." Anything else God wanted to throw in besides would be icing on the cake.

Two and a half years passed. One day in January 1981, I called Father Bill after a session with my spiritual director. After we talked for about an hour, he invited me to dinner the next evening.

Rejoicing, I accepted the invitation. He took me for a romantic meal in the revolving restaurant at the top of the St. Paul Hilton Hotel. Later, he told me that because he did not wish to live alone for the rest of his life, he had made the decision to leave the celibate priesthood, a decision made about two weeks before I called.

Each of us had made our decision alone after much prayer and soul-searching. For this, we thank God, because we did not influence one another's decision. We were married in October; my name changed from Sister Carol to Carol Sisterman.

Bill's mother, Edith, lived with us for a few years after we were married. In 1985, we adopted sibling brothers from Korea. After adopting Charles and Lawrence, we decided that Bill would stay home with them and Edith, who was growing increasingly feeble. After his successful telemarketing years, Bill tried other jobs—carpet salesman, real estate agent, painter. He was unhappy in all of these positions. My work was sporadic too—word processor, teacher, secretary. Our finances were pitiful, but Bill's family helped with adoption costs and house payments. Edith became more feeble and moved to live with Bill's sister on September 13, 1986. Because of my frustration over lack of finances, I threatened divorce more than once. My teaching suffered, and Bill and I both suffered depression. On March 31, 1989, the Thursday after Easter, Edith died, singing, "Joy to the World, the Lord is come; let earth receive her King." The weeks preceding the death of this saintly woman brought major changes to our lives.

Two men from St. Dunstan's Anglican Church in St. Louis Park took Bill to lunch and asked him to pastor that traditional Anglican parish. Because Bill's request for laicization had been denied, he considered this offer. The men asked Bill if I would be willing to take on the life of the wife of an Anglican Catholic priest. I was apprehensive about this, especially since I was teaching in a Roman Catholic school at the time.

However, the following Thursday, Holy Thursday, I was fired. This firing was a dying to the security of the known; I had been unable to admit to myself that by teaching in a Catholic school I could not make sufficient money to support our family.

On Easter Sunday, we went to St. Dunstan's for the first time. For about three months, we attended church there as Bill, incognito, pondered his decision to follow the call. The thoughts that recurred to him were, "They are like sheep without a shepherd," and "They want Eucharist; I do that." Deciding to answer the call, he became their pastor.

Although Bill and I were very angry with the principal and the school board responsible for my firing, I no longer questioned my direction. A window had been closed to my past and a door opened to the future. Within a month of my firing, I was called by a temporary agency to work as a secretary at a law firm where I was later hired. "Your heavenly Father knows all that you need. Seek first his kingship over you, his way of holiness, and all these things will be given to you besides" (Matt 7:32-33).

Carol Deml Sisterman, 1995.
(From a family photo)

Bill's work as a pastor and mine as a legal secretary have been stable. The stability we have gained in answering "yes" to the call of pastoral life gives meaning to our once stumbling, searching existence. Our church community has become the center of our lives. It is where we have made friendships, where our focus is God-centered, where we pray and work together, where we play and laugh as we share meals. Together, in Christ, with Christ and through Christ, we seek God and find peace.

Often people say to me, "Carol, you are so peaceful." I attribute this peace to the life of the Spirit at work within me. The Holy Spirit sparks that peace Jesus gave at the Last Supper: "Peace is my farewell to you, my peace is my gift to you; I do not give it to you as the world gives peace. Do not be distressed or fearful." (John 14:27).

As I look back, major decisions in my life have occurred after prayer, during retreat, or on important liturgical feast days. The Lord has been leading me throughout my life. I do not regret the decision I made to join the convent. I met wonderful people who helped me grow spiritually, emotionally, and intellectually. "God writes straight with crooked lines," is something my Dad used to say. God has certainly done that in my life.

Carol Deml *and Bill Sisterman were married on October 2, 1981. Today, sixteen years later, Bill and Carol are the proud parents of teenage sons, Charles and Lawrence. They live in Hopkins, a suburb of Minneapolis, Minnesota. Together they enjoy gardening, eating Bill's cooking, and ministering to the parishioners of the Anglican Church of St. Dunstan where Bill is pastor.*

Chapter Twenty

Aging's a Lifetime; Maturing's Forever

JoAnn Terhaar White

MID-LIFE LIVING IS A CHALLENGE. Just as you think you've faced various vices as they develop—self-pity, pride, vanity—they seem to reappear like a new strain of virus that has overcome the antibiotic of truth originally applied. During my early years at St. Benedict's, when thinking about the challenges of life was new to me and was as heady as aged wine, I believed that if I just prayed for two things, to learn to love and to know truth, life would be simple and easy. Though I've experienced a running battle with being naive, it didn't take long to learn that life can't be reduced to a couple of spiritual exercises. When one of my many favorite nieces was graduating from college, we decided in our discussion that one of the stimulating aspects of living is that it takes a lifetime to mature. There is always something new to learn, to develop, to overcome that helps to expand one's mind and spirit.

I was the sixth of eight children born to Agnes and Philip Terhaar, good people who lived in a farming community where formal education was of only moderate importance. My parents were intelligent people whose education after eighth grade was influenced by avid reading and the Church. The Church was central in what guided our family, and the driving force in our lives was fear: fear of judgement by God, of those with His earthly authority, of the neighbors, of anyone to whom we gave this power. In this predominantly German, Catholic community, I came to believe that life was based on rules, sex was a tolerated evil, and salvation depended on being a "good person"—mostly just doing what I was told.

I was born September 4, 1941, in Pierz, Minnesota, and three days later baptized JoAnn Mary Terhaar. I attended St. Joseph Grade School and Father Pierz Memorial High School, graduating in 1959. I left this small farming community for a clerical job at BPS Paints in St. Paul the Monday after graduation. Not far from where I lived with six other "home girls" on Marshall Avenue was St. Mark's Parish. Since our apartment had no piano, the nuns at St. Mark's allowed me to practice at the convent. Every weekend we would all go back home to see friends and family. One weekly event for me was teaching piano lessons on Saturdays at St. Joseph's Convent in Pierz to pay off a debt built up for lessons I had received there while in high school.

One Saturday, a former high school superintendent called me into his office and suggested to me that, as I had heard many times before, since I had intelligence, health and was a moral person, I probably had a vocation. After a short discussion, and, being very susceptible to influence by authority, I had, within a week, quit my job, moved everything home and was on my way to test my vocation. If others thought I should do this, then I had an obligation, a duty to do it. It must be God's will. I would choose St. Benedict's since this was my experience of those living convent life. St. Benedict's, St. Joseph, was an oasis of learning, a place to refocus and observe, a new cultural experience, though geographically still in the center of a predominantly German, Catholic community. This oasis community was made up of women with strengths and weaknesses, but with the hint of a direction different from that experienced outside this community.

I entered the Benedictine postulancy with twenty-five other young women in September 1960. After a year of college classes and convent formation classes most of us entered the novitiate where I was given my third choice of new names, Sister Lorna, O.S.B. Being given a new name was a symbol of re-baptism, a new beginning. During the nine years as a "sister" I attended the College of St. Benedict and taught music in grades one through eight at St. Henry's School in Perham and back home in St. Joseph's School in Pierz.

Though the first years in the convent were frustrating, confusing and sometimes depressing for me, it was an experience similar to the many deaths we experience through our lives. Wrenchingly, I changed perspectives on issues. One such never-forgotten example and experience took place during the novitiate. A priest came to address the entire community on the topic, "Loving God in a Personal Way." He gave an impassioned presentation of the realness of such a love. This was frustrating to me. From my previous misguided learning I had closely connected sex and love. How could you love God? Remember, sex was a tolerated vice, and somehow love was connected to it. But how did God's love fit into this?

Another point he made that deeply affected me was the difference in attitudes Northern and Southern Europeans have toward rules. He pointed out that many of the rules of the Church were made by Southern Europeans. Southern Europeans, however, viewed these rules as goals toward which one should aim and, after a lifetime of effort, hope some would be reached. Northern Europeans, however, took the rules as starting points or minimal requirements, to be kept perfectly if at all possible. This was a mind-broadening idea to me and the beginning of a less fearful approach to rules.

Though we certainly were not always quiet during *Magnum Silentium* (the Great Silence), quiet and peace were beginning to seem like worthwhile goals. One of my favorite peaceful places was the St. Benedict's woods, where I first became aware of the simple beauty of nature and our responsibility to protect it. That particular place seemed almost enchanted, a place that encouraged quiet and listening. Even though the Great Silence seemed to be an anachronism, it did serve the purpose of settling down a group of talkative women and giving us the time to focus on why we were there.

During these formative years, the many women doing their life's search via the Benedictine way greatly affected changes taking place in my own life. Prior to this experience, even though I had primarily women teachers, authority and structure in my life were dominated by men. At this time, people of influence in my life were women, intelligent women, prayerful women, women of silence, and women of service. Here were examples of women who proved that they could lead colleges, write books, be renowned artists and researchers, serve on state and national committees. This experience in itself was a new birth for young women attending the college and/or entering their community. These women were not all strong and faultless, but the majority were attempting to live their lives searching for truth and happiness.

Though I was a part of this community for only nine years, significant changes were beginning to take shape within me. I remember a discussion during which someone suggested that some people lived as if a super ego were directing them, telling them what to do. This was a way they could avoid responsibility. I knew everyone must be looking at me, as I recognized myself. Was I really ready to make decisions, follow my conscience, be responsible for my own life? Believe it or not, this was news to me.

As time passed and fears began to recede, questions about the decisions I'd made arose. Was being a nun my decision? At the time I had certainly thought so. But without the paralyzing fears and with a new sense of responsibility, what was truly in my heart and conscience? The reasons for leaving were as varied and complex as those for coming. I had grown in intellectual and spiritual ways and begun the long road to emotional maturity. Rules alone were no longer an end in themselves. A life of thoughtful integrity was a more worthwhile pursuit.

I left the community in June 1969, using the brand new little brown Nova my brother Earl let me use until I could start paying for it. The seeds that were sown in the Benedictine atmosphere I was leaving did take root, and some have flourished into living parts of my life.

First of all, I married Jim, who, because of his warmth and sense of humor, has been good for my soul. Being exposed to humor in my life keeps me from taking myself and what I do too seriously as would be my natural tendency. Married life is a continuing polishing process. Not only do we live together, we travel together and work together in a successful business. With so much togetherness we find the cobwebs, the sharp edges, and the dark places. With a mixture of northern and southern European attitudes, I've learned that the rewards of married life come with the passage of time, of successes and failures, and of difficulties survived.

After leaving the convent, I continued to teach for four years, then traveled for one year with Jim in his college textbook representative job. Then we decided to choose where we wanted to live and find work wherever we landed. We ended up on a park-like 283 acres on the Crow River in Wadena County. Our home is a quiet place with acres of trees and two miles of river where one can find all of the quiet places one could want. Jim loved mathematics, and no sooner had we settled into our new home when the purchase of an income tax franchise became available. Though to some people this seems on the surface to be a business of numbers and cold hard facts, we've always seen it as a service to people who are in a situation each year in which they confront, in their eyes, a gigantic government bureaucracy. We're their buffer. By being as knowledgeable as we are able to be as enrolled agents, we try to simplify this annual obligation for our clients.

Since we have no children, we try to be available to our extended families whenever we can. We have thirty-seven nieces and nephews, some of whom we know well enough to be a special part of their lives. I am impressed by my siblings and their success in raising their children, most of whom have some form of higher education. They are all successful in their own way. As Jim's parents and some childless aunts get older they know they can count on us when needed.

Hospice has been an important volunteer organization for me. Recently I also became involved in the County Parent Aide Program. Since then, two developmentally challenged girls have become a big part of my life. They are now biologically seventeen years old and have serious concerns about their future.

Throughout my life, I've been fortunate to receive the gift of friendship. These friends are good soul searching mates, who, through discussions and insights, help me understand myself.

My spiritual world is important to me and has opened my life to a panoramic inclusion of many influences. For me, "The Church" is all people and all faiths. No one seeker knows all the truths, and all true seekers know some truths from which I can learn. From Christians, I could learn about my responsibilities of living in peace with the people who touch my life and the environment in which I live; from Zen Buddists, simplicity; from Native Americans, a love and respect for nature, and from the B'Hai, being non-judgmental of the journey of all seekers.

JoAnn Terhaar White, 1994. (From a family photo)

This brings me to 1998 at the age of fifty-seven, living quite an ordinary life each day. I cannot say why I am who I am today. I only know I've been touched and influenced by all whom I've met, from my childhood,

125

through my Benedictine experience, my married life and my work experiences. From here I continue on with the hopes of simplifying my life and staying vitally alive as I age and mature. My way continues to be a search for truth and peace.

JoAnn Terhaar White *and her husband, Jim, celebrated their twenty-seventh wedding anniversary in the summer of 1997. Their plans for the future include selling the business they have successfully run for twenty-three years, continuing to work part time for the new owner, and becoming involved in other pursuits. These would probably include volunteering for such organizations as Habitat for Humanity, Vista, and local concerns. They like staying in contact with family and friends (Jim has just discovered e-mail) and also hiding away on their 283 acres of trees, river and space.*

Chapter Twenty-One

A Tapestry in Progress

JUDITH POPP-ANDERSON

BIRTH AND LIFE ARE AWESOME MYSTERIES. My life continues to be a tapestry in progress in which there are many threads that tangle but continue to run through to make a work I do not understand.

November 23, 1943, I was baptized Judith Ann Popp, the youngest child of three born to Harvey and Mary Popp. Family tradition has it that the priest said I would be a fighter for the church. Blessing or planting a seed of hope, church has always been important in my life. I hope that sometimes I have fought for the church. I know at times my spirit has wrestled with the church, but having a relationship with God has prevailed. The church has remained the winner as I continue to treasure her wonderful gifts of Eucharist and social values.

There was never any question about Sunday Mass attendance for Mother and the three kids. There was, however, always a tension on Easter and Christmas because Dad didn't go along. Dad was Missouri Synod Lutheran, and, having attended this church, he would come home singing hymns. He was always supportive of us attending Mass, joined us in not eating meat on Fridays but honestly acknowledged his differences with the faith. Although we were not overly religious, religion was present in our family life.

My first Benedictine influence came when St. Anastasia's parish in Hutchinson, Minnesota, built a parochial grade school. I was in sixth grade at this time and attended sixth, seventh, and eighth grades. The nuns were wonderful. They integrated Christian principles, music, and liturgy into the life and learning process of the school.

I don't know exactly when or how the thoughts of joining the convent came. I know the nuns at the school encouraged it. A cousin and I would play priest and nun instead of house. In the seventh or eighth grade, I received books on various religious orders. The type of habit they wore was the major factor in selecting the one I would join. If they did missionary work they were even more attractive to me.

Sister Nathaniel asked about my going away to Saint Benedict's for high school. My mother was very firm about my being with the family through high school. After that, I could choose for myself. I'm grateful to Mother for that. I certainly think attending public high school fostered my recognition of God present in our world, in everyday events and people. We had release-time religious instruction, getting out of school for an hour to go to our respective churches. All the churches in town participated, and we had some lively discussions afterwards. I probably learned more religion in study hall as a group of us—Baptists, Lutherans, Methodists, and Catholics—argued about our religious beliefs. Ecumenism was beginning to develop.

Through Catholic Youth Club, I became involved in church activities and began to focus more on a need to respond to a call to a religious community. The religious I knew were affirming, accepting and inviting. Their love of God, service, and religious life were almost contagious. The sisters asked me to join them on picnics and various events. In those years, the message that everyone we encounter is Christ was forming deep in my being. I also began to appreciate the improvement in liturgy the Benedictine sisters brought to our parish. Finally, I liked the variety of ministries and involvement in social issues which I discovered to exist among Benedictines.

In 1961 I graduated from high school and spent the summer with friends. Silently, I prayed for cancer or some sign that I shouldn't go to the convent. I knew that without some strong signs from God, I had to give religious life a try. Today, I fully believe listening to that beckoning resulted in gifts beyond measure, including a spiritual foundation for the rest of my life.

In the fall, I entered Saint Benedict's Convent. Leaving me there was an agony for my mother, although she didn't let me know at the time. My sister later shared with me that there were many tears. My brother told me that he was proud of me. Given my personality and tendencies to lose balance and perspective, I recognize how good God was to have me in community rather than in a public university. The cultural impact of that choice is one I continue to embrace with gratitude. "Fight the establishment to create a better world," "God is dead," "If it feels good, do it," were threats of the time, but I could face the culture with God being very real and very much alive. I had a foundation and security in my life.

I do not remember many specifics about convent days. But I do remember threads woven into our lives. Each day as we walked to our postulant refectory the poster, "Life is a journey, not a destination" or "Life is a mystery to be lived, not a problem to be solved" would make me reflect on my lack of freedom of spirit, my taking life too seriously, and my struggling with where I belonged.

The sense of living in the presence of God whether we were in chapel, the bean field, or at recreation began to seep into my soul. The Eucharist tying us to those we loved and to all people became real for me. Christ was the healer of the brokenness of the world. Prayer brought power and peace. Liturgy was nurturing. Easter morning in the novitiate resounded with "This is the day the Lord has made, let us rejoice and be glad in it." Today I can still feel that joy as I try to embrace and live each day, knowing that God has a plan for all of us.

The concept of balance was new to me. Early in our postulancy I was alone one day in our study room when a fellow postulant came to tell me that I had to go to recreation. It didn't make sense to me to do that when I had a Latin test the next day. But now the wisdom of scheduled recreation continues to impress me, especially when I'm the last one to leave the office or I fail to find time for relaxation because work has to be finished first. Balance is a concept I've preached but certainly one I'm a long way from practicing consistently in my life.

I struggled with myself during formation, believing I did not fit or belong in community. I appreciate the gentle assistance and affirmation of my loving superiors. They helped me recognize my goodness, potential, and talent. Although acceptance of that has been a life-long struggle, the community gifted me with hope and some confidence that Christ really has chosen to use me, and I cannot discard that. My life has certainly been richer and more affirmed than I ever believed possible.

When I entered the novitiate I received the name Sister Harvey, a request made in an effort to please my father. Giving up my name was difficult and something I would never do again. In marriage, I kept my own name, hyphenating it before it was a popular thing to do.

It has always been hard for me to break rules, to push limits, and to ask for special favors. The novitiate formation was wonderful, but I fear I could have been too much of a good rule follower and not a strong enough spirit to know which rules to challenge and which to follow. However, formation directors always told me I had leadership potential. Later, bosses would also identify me as a leader.

Sister Harvey Popp, 1964.

The separation from home and the experience in formation did impart some freedom, confidence, and belief that Christ could use me. Cloister served an important role in my life, allowing me to be still and learn that God loves me.

Following a year of Juniorate at Saint Benedict's, I was sent to Holy Angels Grade School in St. Cloud to teach fifth and sixth grades. Although elementary school teaching was certainly not my calling, I had a very rich experience. Since our convent included Cathedral High School teachers, I had the opportunity of being exposed to many sisters living community life. However, I struggled with the feeling of not fitting in, in spite of warm acceptance from nuns of all ages. I learned how truly human nuns are, with strengths and weaknesses, joys and pain.

At Holy Angels I came to face my own decision regarding God's call for me. It was time to renew temporary vows for an additional year. I planned to do that, although I was increasingly sure that mine was not a lifetime religious vocation.

My father was in danger of death that spring, and I was permitted an unusual home visit. Monsignor John Ward, my pastor, had walked with me throughout my earlier struggle and questioning. While home, I visited with him, telling him I had decided to renew temporary vows for one more year although I was still sure this was not God's plan for me. He challenged me, asking what one more year would do, and gave me his acceptance even if I chose to leave.

Amazingly, my father, who had been moved to a metropolitan hospital, received treatment that revealed too much aspirin was causing his internal bleeding. He returned home before we got to Minneapolis to see him.

As I returned to St. Cloud, I pondered my experience of the last years and Monsignor Ward's question; I tried to listen to God and to my heart. It became clear that it was time to leave. In those days, since those decisions were not shared with the community, I told Sister Evin, the house superior, and Mother Henrita, the prioress. I began grieving and crying about all I was leaving. One Sunday in June 1966, several sisters drove me home. I left the community feeling loved and supported but saddened by leaving people about whom I cared and being unable to say good-bye.

I continue to have on my dresser a figurine, Hunger, which a sister friend gave me. Its message is "Empty handed, palms up." It has proven to be a great way to live. That, along with a Benedictine medal paper weight, reminds me daily of the values of my formation. I have always believed it was right for me to go to Saint Benedict's and right for me to leave. The four and one-half years of community life gave me a foundation that has served me and, I hope, God's creation very well.

The colors in the tapestry in my life are very different from anything I expected. One of the gifts has been that half of my maternal aunts and uncles did not marry. Being single was always a very acceptable vocation for our family. I left the community determined to live a dedicated single life.

Benedictine life strengthened my personal relationship with God and others. The practice of living in the presence of God and receiving others as Christ is a peaceful and positive way to live amid the challenges and struggles of our present culture.

"*Ora et labora.*" Prayer and work are central to my life. When I do not spend time in prayer, I tend to spin and lose focus. Work has always been more than a job. It is a vocation, a response to the people and the opportunities God places in my life. As a teacher, social worker, therapist and administrator, I have cried and marveled as I am able to share in the desperation and joys of people's lives. Christ has been present to me in students, in the mentally ill, in alcoholics and other drug addicts, in emotionally disturbed children as well as in family, friends, and co-workers. I have received much more than I have given, seeing men and women on the bottom grow and flourish. My optimism and belief in God's grace working in people is reinforced over and over. I believe that the influence of the Benedictine sisters has been spread to others through me.

I have been blessed with spiritual guides along the way who help me listen to God's direction and, I hope, be obedient to that direction rather than to my own will. That certainly is the case as others helped me wrestle with a vocation to marriage. I had developed a long friendship with an honest man with a beautiful, simple faith. I loved single life and didn't want to be married. However, my prayer, thoughts of God's will, and spiritual direction led me to a marriage commitment on January 10, 1976, to Ruben Anderson.

My marriage has turned out to be a true blessing. Ruben does balance me, being silly and playful, keeping life simple. Having lost his home and family, he treasures ours, keeping me still when I want to be always busy and moving. His journey to communion with the Catholic faith was a quiet one and a great surprise. Being able to share Eucharist is now a great joy.

As noted earlier, balance has always been difficult for me. In 1989 work was not only out of balance; it was my entire life. At my annual physical in November, my doctor recommended a mammogram. Previously, he had said I did not need one for five years, and only a couple of years had gone by. I decided to put it off until one day in January when the doctor's wife, who was a long-time friend and prayer partner of mine, was going in for her second mammogram, having learned that a friend had cancer. Since she was older than I, and this was only her second one, I decided I certainly did not need one. However, I made the appointment. To this day I do not know why I did so,

The mammogram led to a biopsy which revealed cancer. I hadn't thought I had time for the mammogram or biopsy; I certainly didn't have time for cancer. Fortunately, I was on vacation that week so I could spend time in a fog of terror, uncertainty, and prayer. Ruben lovingly journeyed with me. I took many walks with God. What was he asking or telling me?

The year following the diagnosis turned out to be one of the richest of my life, with many lessons. God did not really get my attention right away. That summer, in the midst of chemotherapy, the hospital where I was executive director of the chemical dependency treatment center experienced the longest nursing strike in Minnesota history. Although the treatment center was not as severely affected as the hospital, I felt obligated to function and put in the same hours as other managers.

Ultimately, I crashed. Treatments were finished. Sudden onset of menopause resulted from the chemotherapy, and I was exhausted, depressed and, to use my doctor's words, "a classic case of burnout." For a time, I denied that, believing we are responsible for maintaining balance and caring for ourselves. However, in listening to my body, my spirit, my God, and many who cared about me, I chose to give up my position and take time away from work.

I think of this time as my "mid-life novitiate." In many ways, I structured it like that. I scheduled one to two hours of daily prayer time; went for walks with God; enjoyed lots of solitude, recreation, and spiritual direction. I lived in joy and trust that God had a plan that would unfold. I knew I wanted to embrace life, to say yes to life, and to recapture my spirit.

Lent was wonderful that year, and I planned my own private retreat to experience Holy Week as fully as possible. After that, I would start writing a resumé and investigate the job market. I already had a very clear plan of returning to direct clinical work rather than administration.

On Passion Sunday, my husband noticed an ad for a therapist at the local mental health center. Instead of my well-planned retreat, I filled out an application and civil service forms. I was rewarded with the job of my dreams, where once again I would be able to welcome Christ in the poor and the rich, the deeply religious, and the spiritually bankrupt.

As I reflect on the weaving in my life's tapestry, the benefits of the influence of the *Rule* of Saint Benedict and the Benedictine sisters are evident. Now I am better with balance. I am more consistent in beginning and ending the day in prayer. Most days begin by getting up early for some time of solitude, during which I meditate on the day's Scripture readings, allow Christ to enter my life, and try to experience his presence in the here and now.

Judith Popp-Anderson.

I am thrilled at being a Eucharistic minister both at Mass and for shut-ins. For several years, I had the privilege of coordinating the Rite of Christian Initiation for Adults in our parish. What a joy to journey with people as they come to celebrate Eucharist both at the table and in community.

I remain cancer-free after seven years. I love my life and echo the psalmist's words:

It was you who created my inmost self and put me together in my
mother's womb;
For all these mysteries I thank you; for the wonder of myself, for the
wonder of your works.   Psalm 139

My life is a wondrous, mysterious tapestry, a work in process for the Greater Honor and Glory of God.

Judy Popp-Anderson *has been married to Ruben Anderson since 1976. They make their home in Conger, a small town in southern Minnesota. Together they are proud of Ruben's two sons and are enjoying a granddaughter. Judy, a licensed independent clinical social worker and certified chemical dependency practitioner, currently works as a mental health therapist at Freeborn County Mental Health Center in Albert Lea, Minnesota.*

Chapter Twenty-Two

Tapestry

JAN SALZER

BEING LESBIAN AND ALSO HAVING BEEN a woman religious has woven a rich life tapestry whose warp and woof have been threads of both pain and joy. Denied feelings, depression, isolation, repression, fear of rejection, anger, and oppression were intertwined with sexual aliveness, feeling loving toward and intimate with women, integrating my past, learning to let go, discovering a new voice to speak out, finding new images of spirituality, sexuality, and God, and feeling a new solidarity with the oppressed. This unique tapestry, much of which I wove alone and in ignorance of the process, is an uneven cloth with the warp or woof often pulled off grain. It is shared here so that others may not have to weave theirs in the dark.

I grew up in Minneapolis, the oldest of six children and attended Catholic grade school, high school, and college before entering the community at Saint Benedict's. Having been exposed to prayer, ministry, and community life with women during the many years of Catholic education, I entered Saint Benedict's because I felt called to live those values. As a member of the community for thirteen years, I lived at Saint Benedict's and in several local communities and worked in a variety of ministries including teaching in a middle school and in a high school and working at a home with women, some with children, who are recovering from abuse and drug tendency. As my life process unfolded, these values of prayer, ministry, and community life didn't diminish but took a different focus.

For most of my life I denied my sexual feelings. During my high school and college years and even several years into my religious life, I was only vaguely aware that I was lesbian at the core of my being. Believing that I was asexual because I did not experience the feelings for men that other women described, I assumed that something was missing. When I did allow myself to think about being lesbian, I quickly repressed these sexual thoughts and feelings, which resulted in a loss of most feelings in general. In the consequent numbness, I lived with a constant low-grade depression and felt only pain, fear, and sadness. Rarely could I experience or name any feelings beyond these. Suffering from a lack of self-intimacy and of any real intimacy with others, I could not let anyone get close. This often made living in community difficult.

My sexual awareness and awakening did not come until several years after vowing celibacy. Some years ago when I was in my late twenties, I fell in love with a woman and was utterly terrified. There was no one with whom I could share my feelings of love and fear. There seemed to be no models, no peers to help me discern what was happening, no one with a similar journey against which I could measure my experience. I told my spiritual director of my newly discovered lesbianism and, as I thought at the time, of the insignificance of dealing with the issue because I was celibate. We did not discuss my sexuality again for six months.

During the interim I spent a great deal of time in the library, getting, reading, and hiding stacks of books on homosexuality. I needed to know whether my experience matched what it meant to be lesbian. Some of the images about which I read just did not describe me; the masculine women who wore leather and drove motorcycles definitely did not fit. But images of women feeling tender, loving, and gentle toward other women as well as feeling sexually attracted to them did fit. Deep within myself, I realized I had known my sexual orientation for at least ten years but had been too afraid to acknowledge it consciously. Since I secretly feared being discovered in initial formation, I repressed my feelings and hid behind an outward appearance of harshness and confidence. Indulging in academic pursuits, I developed an overworked head and an underworked heart.

During this time I also vacillated. One day I was certain I was in fact lesbian; the next day, sure that I was not, I was much relieved. I asked lots of questions. Why am I lesbian? Why me? Why is life so difficult? Why me, God? Now I realize that all these questions cannot be answered. I do not know why I am lesbian anymore than heterosexuals understand the *why* of their orientation. I just am, and any attempts at discovering causes seem a waste of time.

But in never sharing my sexual feelings with the woman to whom I was attracted and by never acting on them, I deluded myself, thinking I must not be lesbian. When the object of my affection moved away, I naively thought life would return to "normal" and I would not be attracted to her or any other woman again. Wrong! My sexual feelings remained.

After a great deal of reading and my discovery that my sexual attraction was for more than just *this* woman, I decided to discuss the matter with my spiritual director. Very cautious at first and testing the water for fear of rejection, I was relieved that she was not ignorant, prejudiced or homophobic. She accepted me and helped me with the process of weaving the new tapestry of my life. Some dream work with another spiritual director gave me some rich insights into my sexual attractions and my love for women.

I ventured to tell a friend from another community of my sexual identity. Since she had experienced some difficult times in her life, I sensed that she would understand. At dinner one evening, after skirting the issue with innocuous small talk, I blurted out, "I think I'm a lesbian." She was not shocked or even surprised and, to this day, continues to be a supportive friend.

I tried to find other sisters who were lesbian and finally received one sister's name and met with her. While not too much in our discussion was helpful, largely because each of us was too afraid to say much, at least I then knew that I was not alone.

At this time I also revealed my sexual orientation to one of the sisters with whom I lived because I felt safe and needed some support and encouragement in the house. This was a real saving grace, particularly at times when life seemed unbearable. It was extremely important for me to have a listening ear and moral support in the house where I lived.

As I began coming out to myself and others, I tried to piece together parts of my adolescent years. The things I remembered most were my attraction for an older woman when I was about fourteen, my constant questioning of myself in high school about why I didn't feel the same way about boys as my female friends, liking males as friends but never feeling romantically attracted to them, being kissed by a woman in college and knowing it felt different than a kiss from a family member, being content to stay in the college dorm with women friends rather than dating men. These pieces of my adolescent and early adult years began to enable me to sort out my feelings and identity.

I began to realize that my primary emotional, psychological, social, erotic and spiritual relationships were with members of my own sex, even though I was not overtly expressing these interests, and it was this that made me lesbian. In most respects I was not much different from other community members who receive most of their psychological, emotional, spiritual and social support from other women because religious communities of women are homosocial societies. What makes me and others who are lesbian different at the core of our being, is that we are primarily sexually attracted to women.

Coming out, being able to identify and name my sexual feelings and who I am, was freeing and enabled me to know myself and be known more fully by others. Yet each time I risked sharing my lesbian identity, I had to decide whether another person might construct obstacles toward knowing me because of homophobia, stereotypes, or moral judgments. The cost of possible rejection and perhaps the lack of support of a group of housemates prevented me from sharing my full identity with the larger community. The belief, real or imagined, that I must deny a part of myself to be accepted brought feelings of sadness, but a gift of inner strength and courage sustained me. Since coming out, I have known a greater sureness and purposefulness than I had known before.

At times I was angry with my community for my feelings of not belonging in my total person. I questioned, "If they really knew me, would they still love me?" I also wondered, "Since statistics indicate that at least seven percent of the female population is homosexual, where are the other forty or more lesbian members of my community? Why don't I know anyone else? Are they closeted, on guard and maintaining a facade? Should I keep my inner pain and not be fully known?"

Not without cost, I chose some freedom. I eventually shared my sexual identity with the sisters with whom I lived. But I found little support. I also felt hurt by others who ignored me after discovering my lesbianism. But the subtle oppression of silence about lesbian women religious, which fed my isolation, was the heaviest burden of all.

The Church's stance on homosexuality has been the source of pain and anger for me. By sharing that rage with other church members, I found much reconciliation with these people, whose support helped me realize that love from the church community is far more important than the judgment and prejudice of the hierarchy.

I have also been angry with God and have questioned, "Why me, God? How can you let me endure this? Do you really love me like this? My masculine images of God as father, rescuer, all-powerful ruler and judge had been shattered long ago, and for some time I had felt abandoned. I have a feminine image of God within me. Relating to this image has become a real experience of the Goddess within me, who frees, strengthens, loves, encourages and accepts me unconditionally and gives me a sense of peace.

Peace also came from the support systems with which I was blessed. In addition to a few close friends, I confided in the prioress and most of my work colleagues in order to make intimacy more possible and to prevent me from denying my lesbianism. I also confided in some of my family members who have been wonderfully loving and accepting.

Finally I tried to bridge the void, isolation, and lack of connectedness with other lesbian women in community by belonging to SIGMA (Sisters in Gay Ministry Associated), CCL (Conference of Catholic Lesbians), and Communications, Inc. (an organization of gay and lesbian religious and clergy which publishes a monthly newsletter). Other opportunities to connect with lesbian women religious included support groups, phone networking, and retreats. All of these helped engender a sense of belonging in one's total person to religious community.

Dignity, a support community for gay and lesbian Catholics, which meets twice a month for liturgy and socializing, has been one of the strongest sources of affirmation for me. There I have been free to be myself with other people who, like me, know the joys and sorrows of being gay and lesbian. My experience at a Dignity Retreat, of a deeply loving and holy people, convinced me that never would I believe that gay and lesbian people were evil, or morally or spiritually inferior. The integrated wholeness of spirituality and sexuality in these Dignity members I have not found elsewhere. Many obstacles in the institutional Church and religious community remained. Ultimately, the need to continue to be silent about my identity in the larger community while being out and affirmed elsewhere is what caused me to leave. While there was a rich bonding between community members, there remained a great deal of fear about sexuality and intimacy. When I chose to identify myself as lesbian, it was automatically assumed by some that I was sexually involved. Affection took on sexual connotations. Others denied my existence by claiming that there were no lesbians in our community. Ultimately I found myself saying, "If I stay under these circumstances, my spirit will die."

I left Saint Benedict's in the Spring of 1988, nearly fourteen years after I had entered. Since then, Emma Eskelson and I have made our life's journeys together. We have purchased a house and made a home which we share with many family members and friends. We have two dogs who are our constant companions. Our lives continue to be rooted in those values that brought us to community. Spirituality, community and ministry are still central to our lives.

An active spirituality has called me to help alleviate and direct the pain into ways of overcoming the oppression: speaking, writing, and sitting on various boards and committees. I have spoken about being a lesbian woman to various religious groups, including parish and community justice commissions. I have written bishops concerning the lack of compassion in Church documents and decisions. On boards and committees, I have experienced the rage of God's people at the ecclesial and societal ignorance regarding homosexuality. These groups that have challenged the Chuirch to develop a more liberating theology of sexuality have also decried the hatred that condones abuse and denies people their civil and ecclesial rights.

Jan Salzer.

Through the many people who love and accept me, I have further come to believe that God loves me just as I am. With God's gifts of my sexuality and love of others and through the coming-out process, I have grown from the fear of being gentle and loving to the freedom of gentleness and vulnerability. I can now allow myself to feel closer to other women physically and emotionally and form deeply intimate relationships without fear. Love, affection, and sexual attraction enable me to know myself as lovable and loving. I am grateful to God, the source of that love.

As a lesbian woman gifted with God's love, I believe that I can live out my life and my sexuality consistent with Christ's teach-

140

ings. If Christianity transcends oppressive church systems and is centered in faith communities of God's people, as I believe, then it is possible to be both Christian and lesbian. Being both has enabled me to integrate my spirituality and sexuality as gifts and expressions of God's love for me. To the degree that I share that love and am part of a living, believing community, I am Christian. Christ's ultimate mandate was that all people be loving. I am fortunate to belong to several communities—such as Dignity, my parish, my work group, and a circle of friends—who are striving toward that goal.

Jan Salzer lives in South Minneapolis with her life partner, Emma Eskelson. She continues to work as a house manager at a home for women and children. She enjoys working on home renovation projects and spending time with her family and her dogs. Her present hobbies include needlework and knitting. Her plans for the future are to continue to work against injustices in society.

Cloister walk connecting the chapel to other monastery buildings. (Courtesy of St. Benedict's Monastery archives)

About the Editors

Janice Wedl, OSB, a member of St. Benedict's Monastery in St. Joseph, Minnesota, has been involved in education and administration most of her professional life. Currently she, as a member of the monastery's *Studium*, is a writer of parish histories and is the hospitality hostess for *Studium* guests.

Eileen Maas Nalevanko, a former member of St. Benedict's Monastery, has been involved in nursing education all of her professional life. Among her current interests are reading, fishing, birdwatching, and relaxing as she enjoys the beauty in nature in Minnesota's theatre of seasons.